Lessons from the Vineyard

Lessons from the Vineyard

Developing a Life that's Rich in Character

By Paul E. Sheppard

ISBN-13: 979-8-4881-9437-3

DEDICATION

To my wife, Meredith; my mother, Peggy Sheppard; my son, Aaron; my daughter and son-in-law, Alicia and Jarell; my grandson, Zion; my siblings and their families

To Pastor Kevin Smith and Pastor Lance Lewis, longtime friends who helped me track down the James Montgomery Boice Commentary referenced in this publication

To followers of Christ everywhere who want to build strong character

Table of Contents

Bearing Fruit that Remains

In His parables and sermons, Jesus used down-to-earth examples that His followers could immediately understand about things like farming, fishing, feasts and family. We find one such example in John 15, as Jesus was delivering a significant discourse to His disciples before His crucifixion and resurrection. In this passage are some life-giving lessons from the vineyard:

"I am the true vine and my Father is the vinedresser. Every branch in me that does not bear fruit He takes away; and every branch that bears fruit He prunes, that it may bear more fruit. You are already clean because of the word which I have spoken to you.

"Abide in me and I in you. As the branch cannot bear fruit of itself unless it abides in the vine, neither can you unless you abide in me. I am the vine, you are the branches. He who abides in me and I in him bears much fruit; for without me you can do nothing." — John 15:1-5

I love how Jesus uses an agricultural metaphor to make His point. His words are so powerful because truth runs parallel in the physical and spiritual. When you see truth in the physical realm, you can trace it to corresponding truths in the spiritual realm.

Here Jesus is talking about grapevines and how He is the true vine and His Father is the gardener. His Father owns the vineyard. Then Jesus draws each one of us into that vineyard saying, "I am the vine, you are the branches." He connects all of His people to the vine.

We are the branches. We will succeed in the purpose for which we have been created, as long as we are connected to the true vine. That's the key. The life we now live is not our own, since we were crucified with Christ (Galatians 2:20). Our life comes through Christ, the life-giving vine. As a result, we will bear much fruit. This fact should motivate us to make our lives count here on earth. He has made a way for our lives to count, since we are His fruit-bearing people in the world.

Jesus did not come to establish a religion. He never told His disciples "Follow me because I'm establishing the world's greatest religion." No, no! He came to connect us to the Father. He came to make sure that our lives are the best that they can possibly be, because of our connectedness with the Father.

Go back one chapter to John 14 and Jesus tells us how to be connected to the Father. He said:

"I am the way, the truth and the life. No one comes to the Father except through me." — John 14:6

Jesus is the way. He is the truth. He is the life. Because of Jesus, we are connected to the vine, which means we will produce much fruit. This connectedness gives us purpose. It brings meaning to life. It means we are connected to something much bigger than ourselves.

Genuine Fruit — Jesus is the Real Deal

The first lesson from John 15 is this: Jesus is the real deal. He's the true vine. He's not pretending. He is the Son of God. He is the life-giver. He is the true vine.

The implications for us are unmistakable. We can't be phony and connected to the true vine. We can't be fake and plugged into true love and truth and righteousness.

This fact ought to make us want to live high-quality, genuine lives in Christ. We should want the real thing, not phoniness. We should be sick of fooling with phony people, as if they have anything we need. We should want more of Jesus, the real deal, not fake imitations. We don't want cheap facsimiles. We want the real thing.

Choose substance over style. Style is fine, but substance is essential. Spiritual style is having a big Bible, looking holy and saying, "Praise the Lord." Style is fine but don't try to present yourself as something you're not. Be authentic. Live on the strength that you draw from the vine. Don't content yourself with trappings. Don't be all sizzle and no steak. Don't make a show of religious language without the faith and love and devotion and sacrifice to back it up. Go for the real deal.

Jesus set us up for success. He connected us to the source of everything we could ever need. He set us up to succeed, but not by the world's standard. Success in the Kingdom of God has very little to do with status, power, a nice house and car, and a high-paying career. Yes, it's possible to serve God with the worldly trappings of success, but know that they often get in the way. Heaven's definition of success is a lot different than cars and cribs and cash.

Here's what God told Joshua about success:

"This Book of the Law shall not depart from your mouth but you shall meditate in it day and night, that you may observe to do according to all that is written in it. For then you will make your way prosperous and then you will have good success." — Joshua 1:8

Heaven's definition of success means getting plugged into God's word and doing His will, day and night, in season and out of season.

Jesus is the real deal.

The world around us wants to blend all religions together, saying they're all true. And yet Jesus said, "I am the way." He didn't say, "We are the way," or "I am one of the ways." He said, "I am *the* way, *the* truth and *the* life."

Yes, we love all people of every faith, but we don't lump our beliefs together in one big hodgepodge. We cannot blend Jesus with Muhammad and Buddha and Krishna and Confucius and all the others. We love and value all people equally, but Jesus stands apart and above. He is not "one of the ways." He is *the way*. He said, "No man comes to the Father but by me."

Jesus is the real deal.

If you want to question the claims of Jesus, hold Him up to all the other spiritual leaders and prophets. How many of them died for their people and then rose from the dead?

None of them.

All the other religious leaders died. You can visit their tombstones. But Jesus rose again, showed himself alive for 40 days and then ascended to heaven with the promise of coming back soon. Not only that, but He's coming back for a church without spot or wrinkle (Ephesians 5:27), so we must be ready to meet Him. We need to share His love and truth with as many people as possible so they can join the family of Christ.

We cannot be so ecumenical that we try to blend Jesus with all the other claims to truth. If someone says, "Well, Jesus was just a prophet, like all the other religious leaders," we need to say, "Actually, that's not what Jesus said."

When you look at the testimony of Jesus, you will conclude that either He is the real deal or He was the greatest phony that ever lived. Jesus made some bold claims. He said He was God. He said, "Before Abraham was, I am" (John 8:58). Not only was He claiming to have been alive before Abraham, but He was using a sacred name — *I am* — that only God could use about Himself. When God sent Moses to free the Israelites from Egypt, He said, "Tell them '*I am*' sent you" (Exodus 3:14). The Jews who were listening to Jesus instantly recognized that He was claiming to be God by calling Himself "I am." That's why they tried to stone Him to death in the very next verse, although the Bible says He hid Himself from them (John 8:59).

Ordinary prophets do not say that kind of thing, especially if they'll get executed for blaspheme. Somebody who makes that kind of claim is either crazy or God. Anyone who reads the claims of Jesus must conclude that He was either a complete lunatic or He is the real deal.

When Jesus says He's the true vine in John 15, He is being consistent with what He's been saying all along. He is calling us to be connected with the true vine so that we can bear genuine fruit.

When I was preaching this message at our church, I stepped down from the podium carrying an attractive little basket of fruit. If you had skipped breakfast that morning, your mouth would have been watering at the sight of those yellow bananas, red apples and delicious looking oranges.

"Have some fruit," I said to the congregation. "Anybody who's hungry, grab it and eat it. Take some of my fruit, brothers and sisters."

So, they took me up on my offer and grabbed some of the fruit. That's when one of the brothers said, "Pastor, we can't eat this."

"What's the problem?" I asked.
"It's fake," he said.
"Fake?"
"It's not real."
"It's not real?" I said. "Now that is a problem."
It sure looked shiny and delicious, though. The problem

is …

…the fruit was fake.

You can't eat fake fruit. You can put it in a bowl and make an attractive decoration but it will never sustain you when you're weak and in need of nourishment.

In the same way, the world doesn't need phony Christians. Fake fruit won't nourish anybody. The world needs the real deal. They need believers with genuine fruit.

Hear Jesus saying, "Don't sell me short by being a phony. Don't tell the world about a genuine Savior while being a phony follower. I am the true vine so bear genuine fruit. You can't represent a true vine with fake fruit."

Fruitful Living is Important to God

In John 15, Jesus shares lessons from the vineyard with His disciples. In the opening verses, we have seen how Jesus is the true vine and we are the branches. We have seen how that connectedness enables us to bear genuine fruit. Let's see now what Jesus says in verse 16:

> *"You did not choose me but I chose you and appointed you that you should go and bear fruit and that your fruit should remain, that whatever you ask the Father in my name He may give you."* — John 15:16

This passage reminds me of one of the songs I heard when I was growing up. The title was "I've Decided to Make Jesus My Choice." A lot of people feel as if the "decision" to follow Jesus was all theirs. They feel as if they were acting on their own volition when they responded to an invitation from a preacher. And yet here we see Jesus saying, "You did not choose me but I chose you."

The fact is, you would have had no choice if He hadn't first chosen you.

When God sent His Son, He chose you.

You didn't choose Him; He chose you.

People say, "I found the Lord back in 1997." The reason you "find something" is because it's lost, and just for the record ... Jesus wasn't lost in '97. That's when He *found you.* That's when He brought you home. That's when He reached out to you. That's when you responded to His choosing you.

I make this distinction, first, to remind us to be humble and grateful that while we were yet sinners, Christ died for us (Romans 5:8). The Holy Spirit was pursuing us. The Father was reaching out to us in love. And secondly, it's important to acknowledge the purpose of God in choosing us.

What purpose?
To bear fruit.
To be fruitful.
You didn't choose me. I chose you and appointed you that you should go and bear fruit ...

Moreover, we are connected to the True Vine so that we won't bear phony, decorative fruit.

... and that your fruit should remain ...

Genuine fruit *remains*. It nourishes. It pleases. It produces a plentiful harvest. It has a positive impact.

Being fruitful means living a high-quality life, which is what Jesus commissioned us to do. Being fruitful means having character traits that are real, not cheap and fake. It means making life count. It means making life good. It means making it high quality. It means bearing high quality fruit that remains.

How, specifically, do we bear fruit?

We bear fruit through fruitful actions as a result of good works. Jesus said:

"A good man out of the good treasure of his heart brings forth good things ..." — Matthew 12:35

When Jesus saves us, He transforms us on the inside. He produces a good treasure in our hearts and out of that treasure comes the good things He has ordained for us to do. Out of that treasure comes the high-quality fruit we are appointed to bear.

No believer should have a heart that wants to do evil. If evil is in you, go to the Lord and say, "God, give me a clean heart." Be like David who repented of his sin and prayed before the Lord:

Create in me a clean heart, O God and renew a steadfast spirit within me. — Psalm 51:10

God can only work righteousness from the inside out. He can't make genuine fruit out of fake materials. If your righteousness is only external, you are not the real deal. You are like the Pharisees who had an external righteousness, which God said was like filthy rags (Isaiah 64:6).

The Lord didn't come into your life to do a superficial makeover. He placed a good treasure in your heart so you can bring forth good things. What kind of relationship do you have with evil? Are you troubled by the things in your life that don't align with God's will? Or are you working to rid your life of these things? Nobody is perfect, but God's people should never be happy about wrongdoing. When God is at work in your heart, you will be troubled by things that are out of His will.

The Apostle Paul wrote:

And let our people also learn to maintain good works, to meet urgent needs, that they may not be unfruitful. — Titus 3:14

As you can see, this theme of fruitfulness comes up over and over again in God's word. Here Paul is saying that fruitful lives are characterized by good works and meeting urgent needs. Jesus calls Christians to represent His heart of compassionate. Uncompassionate believers need a heart transplant.

When you have the heart of God, you cannot help but respond to the urgent needs around you. That's why He gifted you with time and abilities and resources. You can't help everybody but you can help some.

Meet the urgent needs … so you will not be unfruitful.

Unfortunately, believers are accustomed to conditioning themselves with a whole list of excuses. "The problem is too big. There are too many people hurting. Besides, those folk begging for money are all phonies."

How do you know their hearts? Sure, some are running a scam, but they can't be that rich if they're sitting in the dirt at the freeway exit. That's not the path to prosperity. If you're not positive it's a scam, then say, "Lord, what do you want me to do here? How can I represent you here?"

I know how folks can roll. I don't want to fund somebody's drug. I won't give someone money if I think they're going to use it for the wrong thing. But if they're hungry, I'll help them get something to eat. I'll go with them and pick up a hamburger, because that's an urgent need.

If they have an urgent need, represent the heart of God to them. Let them "taste and see that the Lord is good" (Psalm 34:8). Let the love of God fill their belly. Help folk who are struggling so they don't have to fall into poverty or homelessness. And if you don't have anything material to give them, at least you can give them some respect and a smile.

That's one way to make sure you are being fruitful, by making a habit of good works. You can't meet every need all the time. Sometimes all you have to offer is a smile and a prayer. But never forget what it says in Ephesians 2:10:

For we are His workmanship, created in Christ Jesus for good works, which God prepared beforehand that we should walk in them. — Ephesians 2:10

You were *created for good works*. Before you were born, God had some things for you to do. *Good works* are part of your job description on planet Earth. It's your purpose, so don't leave Earth without finishing your chores. Don't leave here with an unfulfilled calling. Like Jesus said in John 15, "I appointed you to go forth and bear fruit." We bear fruit in our works and we bear fruit in our character. So bear genuine fruit. Feed and nourish people from your good works. Leave a positive impact. Leave people behind you who are well-nourished because of the fruit you share. Make their lives better because of the good things that come from the Holy Spirit in you.

Live a fruitful life and the people around you will be blessed by the overflow of your emotional, physical and spiritual nutrients.

Three Levels of Bearing Fruit

In John 15, Jesus taught that there are three levels of bearing fruit. In verse two, He said:

"Every branch in me that does not bear fruit He takes away; and every branch that bears fruit He prunes, that it may bear more fruit." — John 15:2

Here we see the first two levels of bearing fruit, which include bearing *no fruit* and bearing *more fruit*. We see the third level of bearing fruit in verse five:

"I am the vine, you are the branches. He who abides in me and I in him bears much fruit; for without me you can do nothing." — John 15:5

The three levels of bearing fruit are:

- *bearing no fruit*
- *bearing more fruit*
- *bearing much fruit*

This message is for everyone. It's for those who have just gotten connected to the vine and want to begin bearing fruit. Also, it's for those eager to bear more and much fruit. There's something here for everybody.

Maybe you feel as if you're <u>bearing no fruit</u> at all. Maybe you're saying, "I asked the Lord into my life some time ago, but I still don't see much difference in my life. Not a lot has changed. I accepted Christ as my Savior but I still feel like the same person. As far as I can tell, I'm not bearing fruit."

If that's you, first let me congratulate you for being honest enough to admit it. Your honesty enables you to move to a better place. Unfortunately, too many congregations are communities of condemnation, excelling at making sure you know you don't measure up. They constantly insist that God is very unhappy with your shortcomings, and so are they.

The church is not supposed to treat you like the accused in a courtroom. The church is supposed to be a hospital where sin-sick people experience forgiveness, salvation, and healing. People don't go to the hospital to show off how perfect they are. They go because they are hurting and in need of both healing and human compassion. People don't apologize for being sick at the hospital. It's okay to be honest about your problems in a hospital, and so it should be at church. Nobody will get better if they're in denial about their sicknesses.

Churches need to be places where it's okay to say, "I don't see any fruit in my life. I've always been an ill-tempered person but I want to change. I've been lustful but I don't want to be remain that way. I've been stingy. I have bad attitudes toward certain people in my life. I'm struggling with unforgiveness. I don't see godly fruit growing in my life."

When I hear words like these from frustrated believers, I respect and admire their honesty as well as their willingness to admit that things need to change. You cannot be phony and get where God wants to take you. You cannot change what you refuse to confront. I thank God for those who are willing to admit they don't see any fruit in their lives.

Jesus is the true vine, and He calls us to bear genuine fruit. That means we will be eager to bring healing to our brothers and sisters, nurturing them so they can move from a place of unfruitfulness to a place of bearing much fruit. We stand together as His church, encouraging each other to move from where we are to where He has destined us to be.

He Lifts Up the Branches with no Fruit

In verse two, many bible translations say that He "takes away" the branches that bear no fruit. This phrase confuses some people because it suggests that such branches are good for nothing. But in actuality, the Greek word *airo* may be rendered, "lifts up." Could this be the key to understanding the verse? Could Jesus have said that if a branch is bearing no fruit, the gardener *lifts it up* where sunlight, rain, and heat can cause fruit to develop on the vine?

In my view, this translation of the word *airo* clears up any confusion about what Jesus meant. It eliminates the idea that God cuts off true believers and disallows them to remain in relationship with Him. Rather, it tells us that if we are presently unfruitful, our Lord will provide the love, grace, and spiritual enrichment we need in order to bear fruit.

He lifts them up.

To deepen your understanding of this truth, I'd like to share a conversation that Pastor Bruce Wilkinson had with the owner of a large vineyard in Northern California:

> *"New branches have a natural tendency to trail down and grow along the ground," [the vineyard owner] explained. "But they don't bear fruit down there. When branches grow along the ground, the leaves get coated in dust. When it rains, they get muddy and mildewed. The branch becomes sick and useless."*
>
> *"What do you do?" I asked. "Cut it off and throw it away?"*
>
> *"Oh, no!" he exclaimed. "The branch is much too valuable for that. We go through the vineyard with a bucket of water looking for those branches. We lift them up and wash them off." He demonstrated for me with dark, callused hands. "Then we wrap them around the*

trellis or tie them up. Pretty soon they're thriving." —
from *Secrets of the Vine,* by Bruce Wilkinson [1]

If you are a frustrated believer who is bearing no fruit at
the moment, please stop beating yourself up. God has a
purpose, not just for wonderfully fruitful people, but for
you as well. He will complete the work He began in you.
You may not look like much right now, but He has
ordained your destiny. He loves you as you are, but He will
not leave you as you are. He wants to lift you up and
expose you to the cleansing sunlight.

Since God does not condemn you, don't condemn
yourself. And don't accept as valid the condemnation of
others. Go to a church that affirms the truth of who you are
in Christ; a church that gives you hope. Surround yourself
with Christians who do not constantly heap condemnation
on you. Things might not look great right now, but just
keep your hand in the Lord's hand. He will bring you up
and He will bring you out of unfruitfulness!

The renowned biblical scholar Dr. James Montgomery
Boice, who pastored Tenth Presbyterian Church in
Philadelphia, explained why the translation "lift up" from
John 15:2 is superior:

*First, the emphasis [is] upon the care of the vine by the
Father. It would be strange, granting this emphasis, if
the first thing mentioned is the carrying away of
unproductive branches. But it is not at all strange to*

---

[1] Bruce Wilkinson, *Secrets of the Vine: Breaking Through to
Abundance* (Colorado Springs: Multnomah Books,
2001), 33-35.

emphasize that the gardener first lifts the branches up so that they may be better exposed to the sun and so the fruit will develop properly ... It would be a strange gardener who immediately cuts off such a branch without even giving it a chance to develop properly. But it would be wise and customary for him to stretch the vine on an arbor or use some other means of raising it to the air and sun.[2]

Know that God wants you to grow and thrive. Don't beat yourself up if you don't see much fruit. Don't let the devil say, "You know you're supposed to be a Christian, but look at you. You're all messed up."

That's like criticizing people in the hospital for being sick. You don't do that! They checked in because they were sick. They are right where they need to be so the physician can begin the healing process.

You know you're in the right place when your raggedy bits are exposed to the sunlight of God's love. Hold them up to His word. Be encouraged and edified by His people. You might feel condemned but let it slide. That's not from God. When you are in His word and surrounded by His people, know that you are in the right place. You are being lifted up to God's healing light. You're in the right place.

God loves you too much to leave you down in the mold and the mud. He created you to be a healthy branch. He wants to lift you up, so be encouraged. You might not feel very holy but that's okay. You might not feel very spiritual

---

[2] James Montgomery Boice, *The Gospel of John, An Expositional Commentary, Volume 4* (Grand Rapids: Baker Books, 1985; 1999), 1161-1162.

but don't let your feelings take control. Know that as long as you remain in the vine, God will be accomplishing His plan for you. God will be working to bring His purpose to your life. Keep fellowshipping with godly people. Keep exposing yourself to His word. Keep reading books like this one. Know that His word never returns void (Isaiah 55:11). He will bring beautiful fruit to your life.

I'll never forget a man I once met at church who was under a heavy load of condemnation.

"How can we be praying for you?" I asked.

He said, "I don't think I can be saved."

"Why not?" I asked.

"Some people are predestined to be lost and go to hell," he said, "and some are predestined to be saved. I think I'm one of those who are predestined to be lost."

"Why would you even think that?" I asked. "God wants all people to be saved."

He said, "I just can't get my life together. I think I'm supposed to be lost."

"Let me help you understand something," I said. "If you were that kind of person, guess what? You wouldn't be here crying at the altar."

Even if someone is choosing to go buck wild in his sins, it's not irrefutable evidence that God has destined him for hell. Scripture clearly states that God "desires all men to be saved and to come to the knowledge of the truth" (1 Timothy 2:4). Yes, hell is a reality. When people complain and say, "I don't believe a loving God would send people to hell," I agree with them. Why? Because He doesn't send you there! If you're going to hell, it's because you bought the ticket. The destination is your choice. You set your own course toward hell.

That reminds me of a story an older friend told me about his first day as a student at Germantown High School in Philadelphia in the 1960s. School faculty members were handing out rosters for the classes when my friend heard an older student say, "You better hope you don't see the name *Gadlock* on your class roster, because that lady doesn't play! She stands about six feet tall and weighs in around 200 pounds. You don't want to be in Mrs. Gadlock's class."

Of course, my friend looked at his roster and indeed saw the name *Gadlock*. He said that nervousness set in as he began to imagine a long, dreadful school year.

When it was time for his first class with her, he made sure he was in the classroom before the final bell rang. "When the teacher walked in," my friend said, "she looked just like they said. A big, bad sister. Then she looked at us and said, 'My name is Mrs. Gadlock. You probably heard a lot of things about me. You probably heard that I don't take foolishness," she said, "and that is absolutely true. If you start something in this class, I'm going to finish it!'"

My friend sat there looking up at her, trying to conceal the nervousness he felt. "I actually heard that she had decked a couple of dudes," he told me. Of course, this was the 1960s, when corporal punishment was legal in public schools. My friend didn't know if it was true, but the rumor was that she decked a couple of students who defied and disrespected her.

Then Mrs. Gadlock said, "I'm sure you've also heard that I flunked more people than you can name, but that's not true. I need to clear the air over that misrepresentation of me."

This actually shocked my friend, who was himself afraid of getting flunked. "I haven't flunked anyone," Mrs. Gadlock explained. "If you flunk, you will have flunked yourself. I'm a good teacher. I go to great lengths to give you all the information you need. I even make myself available at recess or after class to explain things. I want to help you succeed. There is no reason why you should flunk my class. So if you flunk, don't blame it on me. *You will have flunked yourself.*"

As it is in the natural, so it is in the spiritual. If you're planning on going to hell, don't say that God sent you there. If you reject His love — if you reject His grace — don't put it on God's shoulders. You will have sent yourself there.

Jesus did not come to bring condemnation.

God so loved the world that He gave His only begotten Son, that whoever believes in Him should not perish but have everlasting life. For God did not send His Son into the world to condemn the world, but that the world through Him might be saved. — John 3:16-17

God does not condemn you, so stop condemning yourself. If you flunk the test, you will have flunked yourself. If you feel as if you are bearing no fruit, submit to the Father's care. Let Him lift you up and bring you to a better place. He doesn't hate you. He loves you. He is at work in your heart. The fact that you're sitting under the word means you are moving in the right direction.

Don't let the devil talk you out of your destiny. God is doing beautiful things in your life. If it seems as if you're not bearing fruit right now, that doesn't mean you're not going to bear fruit. Stick with the Lord. Stick with His plan for your life. Abide in Him and He will lift you up.

He Prunes the Branches that have Fruit

I should have warned you that this isn't a shouting and dancing message. When I preach this message in church, I don't hear a lot of "hallelujahs" because people aren't giddy and giggling about getting pruned.

In John 15:2, Jesus said, "Every branch that bears fruit He prunes." This is the second level of bearing fruit.

Pruning is not fun. It can even be painful. Pruning cuts you — not to destroy you, but to make you better. The Lord takes branches that are bearing some fruit and He prunes them because He wants them to bear more fruit. He cuts so that you'll do better once He's finished pruning you.

The vineyard dresser knows that some of the unnecessary material will hinder the fruitfulness of that vine. His careful pruning will cause the vine to not only bear more fruit but to bear better fruit. The fruit that remains will be sweet and ripe and luscious. The vinedresser knows how to improve both the quantity and quality of the fruit. So even if a branch is already bearing fruit, the farmer might still prune it to produce better fruit.

I'm not a gardener but I learned these truths in my study. I don't do dirt. God bless all you gardeners who like to put on your floppy hats and stick your fingers in the dirt. Personally, I don't do dirt. The closest I get to gardening is in books. But I'm glad you like all that digging, so knock yourself out. Enjoy yourself and know that people like me love the fruit of your labor. I love to see beautiful flowers. I love to eat luscious fruit. But trust me when I say you don't want me helping you. My wife knows not to leave flowers in my care because I will kill them. She says, "Why didn't you water that plant? Didn't you see that it was dying?" And I say, "Huh …?" Long ago, she learned not to leave a healthy plant with me and expect it to be alive when she gets back home.

I'm a pastor.
I do funerals.
I don't do gardens.

Still, I learned a lot about vines and pruning when I was studying the deeper spiritual lessons from the vineyard. The purpose of pruning is to bring the plant to its optimal potential. It is a means of accessing the richness and purpose of the vine.

In the spiritual realm, we see how the Lord's chastening relates to the metaphor of pruning. This principle is expanded upon in Hebrews 12:

> *And you have forgotten the exhortation which speaks to you as to sons: "My son, do not despise the chastening of the Lord, nor be discouraged when you*

*are rebuked by Him. For whom the Lord loves He
chastens and scourges every son whom He receives."*

*If you endure chastening, God deals with you as
with sons; for what son is there whom a father does not
chasten? But if you are without chastening, of which all
have become partakers, then you are illegitimate and
not sons. Furthermore, we have had human fathers who
corrected us and we paid them respect.*

*Shall we not much more readily be in subjection to
the Father of spirits and live? For they indeed for a few
days chastened us as seemed best to them, but He for
our profit, that we may be partakers of His holiness.
Now no chastening seems to be joyful for the present,
but painful; nevertheless, afterward it yields the
peaceable fruit of righteousness to those who have been
trained by it.* — Hebrews 12:5-11

Here we see how God ordained the principle of
chastening so that His people might reach their maximum
potential.

*... afterward it yields the peaceable fruit of
righteousness ...*

Here's an important spiritual truth: *Optimal potential
sometimes takes subtraction.* Spiritual growth is not all
about addition. Godly rebuke can bring positive results.

These days, many people want to be affirmed, affirmed,
affirmed all the time. Without question, affirmation is
positive, but it *alone* will not bring you to your maximum
potential and development. To become the woman or man
of God that you were created to be, you can't expect

everybody to make you feel wonderful all the time. God didn't design things to work that way. He planned for you to grow through discipline and even rebuke. He wants you to hear Him say, "This is not my plan for you. We need to prune some things here. You need to get rid of some things here so you will fulfill my optimum purpose."

I think of the naïve teen who gets fed up with mom and dad's rules and says, "I'm sick of this. I'm joining the army." I've seen it happen. They run off dreaming of a better life, then before long they're wishing to God they were back home. At 3:30 in the morning, they're already running 100 miles with a pack on their back, with not a bite to eat until after several hours of grueling sweat and blisters. Trust me; nobody is cheering them on and affirming them, saying "You're so awesome. Look at you go! You doing alright now? How are you feeling? We sure hope you're enjoying the morning air. Anything we can get to make you feel more comfortable?"

The fact is, nobody cares if you enjoy running. Nobody cares about your feelings. All that matters is that they're helping you become the best that you can possibly be.

God prunes our branches so they'll bear better fruit. If you're looking for an apology, I'm afraid you will be disappointed. *It is what it is.* And to many people, it's an uncomfortable fact of the spiritual life. Be encouraged that you are in good hands. Your Father loves you and He knows what He's doing. He will prune you to maximize the fruitfulness of your life.

Four Areas of Pruning

What does it mean to be pruned?
Pruning is God's way of getting rid of some stuff.
What does He want to get rid of?

God wants to get rid of some *people*, some *places*, some *practices* and some *priorities*. And as we have seen, this process is often uncomfortable.

In some cases, *God* cuts things away. You don't plan to get rid of something or someone, but suddenly it's gone. In other cases, it's up to *you* to prune off something that doesn't belong in your life. You know how difficult it can be when God gets rid of some people, places, priorities or practices that you like. When that happens, you wonder what's going on.

God is pruning you.

God will send some **people** out of your life, whether they are Christian or not. He will send them away and you might not even know why they left. Your feelings might be hurt and your ego bruised. You might wonder how anyone could leave you, as wonderful as you are. This may come as a news flash, but God never intended to leave you "as you are." Sure, He sees some fruit in your life, but He wants to cultivate you so you can bear much fruit. And in order to do that, He has to get rid of some people in your life.

He will get rid of some **places** in your life. He will close some doors.

God will get rid of some **practices**. He will lead you to change some of your activities and habits.

He will get rid of some **priorities**. He will gradually transform your way of thinking.

Don't assume that something has to be sin for God to prune it from your life. He didn't say it had to be sin for Him to get rid of it. The vinedresser is not just looking for sick or weak branches to cut. He's also looking for healthy branches that are getting in the way. His intent is to make the vine as fruitful as possible and that means cutting back all different kinds of branches.

Not everything that God prunes in your life will be sinful or bad. In His best purpose and plan, He may want to trim something good from your life. The Apostle Paul understood this when he wrote:

All things are lawful for me but all things are not helpful. All things are lawful for me but I will not be brought under the power of any. — 1 Corinthians 6:12

God in His wisdom knows what's best for you. He chooses to cut some things back, even if they are not sinful. Sometimes He will say, "This is not for you because in time, I know that you will come under the power of it. It's not sin but it has the potential of controlling you."

Christians often argue, "I'm going to do this thing because you can't show me in the Bible where it's sinful." That's the wrong approach to take because God says, "Sometimes it's not about sin. There are things you shouldn't do because they hinder my best in your life."

This principle is so important that Paul repeated it in 1 Corinthians 10:

All things are lawful for me but not all things are helpful; all things are lawful for me but not all things edify. — 1 Corinthians 10:23

You might ask God, "How does this hurt me?" Instead, hear God saying, "But how does it help you?" You can't argue with God, claiming something is lawful when He is saying it's not helpful. You can't defend your actions, saying you can still go to heaven and do this thing. That's not the question. God's goal as your spiritual vinedresser is to make you fruitful here on earth before you get to heaven.

To be most fruitful here, some things need to go. Some people have to go. Some practices have to go. Some priorities have to go. Some places have to go. This is God's plan for our best.

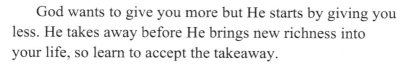

Pruning is subtraction that results in addition.

God wants to give you more but He starts by giving you less. He takes away before He brings new richness into your life, so learn to accept the takeaway.

We have been talking about the times when God takes away, but just as important are the times when it's up to you to walk away from something ... and that's not always comfortable. You hear God asking you to get rid of some things and you don't like it because it's not going to be easy.

The pain of pruning is obvious in the story of Hagar

and Ishmael, the servant girl and natural son born to Abraham. In Genesis 21, Abraham's wife Sarah got upset at Ishmael for mocking his half-brother Isaac when he was about two years old, at the time of his weaning. When Sarah saw that teenaged knucklehead messing with her baby, she stomped over to Abraham and said, "That boy has got to go."

Abraham said, "Baby, that's my son Ishmael. You know how he came to be when ... well, you remember. You came up with that scheme for me to have a baby with Hagar."

"Thanks for reminding me," Sarah said, "She's gotta go too. Get the both of them gone. Now!"

This was not a negotiation. This was not a discussion. It was a done deal.

So Abraham went to God and said, "Lord, what am I gonna do? There's nothing but thirsty desert out there. I can't just send them away, can I?"

And the Lord said, "Listen to your wife."

Hmm ... That's strange advice from a God who is known as the defender of the weak (Psalm 82:3). And yet He never said He was going to abandon them. He never said one party was innocent and the other was guilty. He only said, "Listen to your wife. Pack up some provisions and send them away. It's time for them to go."

Imagine the pain of this single mother and her teenage son. They must have had so many questions, and yet as the story unfolds, we see God send an angel to minister to them and provide for their needs. We see how God gives them a home and blesses them. He was pruning and providing a better life for them in the days ahead.

This story has practical applications for our lives today. You know how tough it is when God says that some people ought not to be in your life. You wonder how you'll survive after they're gone. Maybe you have more than one Ishmael that has to go. There's an Ishmaela. And an Ishmaelika. God is saying, "Pack them all up. Give them some provisions. Let them go, once and for all, with no regrets."

Maybe it's your firstborn who needs to learn how to stand on his own two feet. Maybe it's a codependent relationship. If God wants you to let them go, then let them go. Put some provisions on their shoulders, hug them, tell them you love them and send them out the door. God can take care of them from there.

You say, "It's gonna be painful" and you're right. And yet to be obedient, you have to cry sometimes. You have to let some things go. But know that while God is pruning, He shares your pain. He will not put more on you than you can bear. It won't be easy. You may even say, "Lord, you're killing me!" But you're not going to die. He's only getting rid of the things that will hurt you in time. He's pruning you so that you can bear much fruit.

Pruning is an inevitable part of the Christian life. Nobody learns to walk without falling a few times. Everybody experiences set-backs on the road to success. Thank God for His pruning. Thank God that He lifts us up.

This is one of the most important lessons we learn from the vineyard.

Abide in Me

As we return to the main text from John 15, take special note of the repetitive phrases in these five verses:

"Abide in me and I in you. As the branch cannot bear fruit of itself unless it abides in the vine, neither can you unless you abide in me. I am the vine, you are the branches. He who abides in me and I in him bears much fruit; for without me you can do nothing. If anyone does not abide in me, he is cast out as a branch and is withered; and they gather them and throw them into the fire and they are burned. If you abide in me and my words abide in you, you will ask what you desire and it shall be done for you. By this my Father is glorified, that you bear much fruit; so you will be my disciples." — John 15:4-8

In this short section, Jesus says "abide" a total of seven times. Why is He so repetitive?

So we don't miss it!

Here Jesus repeatedly offers us the key to fruitful living.

Abide in me.

Before we unpack the practical aspects of *abiding*, we

must establish one crucial point: This section of scripture is not intended to be twisted and used as a warning against the fires of hell. A legalistic segment of Christianity gains a perverted sense of pleasure in consigning folks to hell. They see the word "fire" and images of hell come into their heads. They say, "If you're not bearing fruit, you're going to burn. Watch out, 'cuz the flames of hell are already licking at your heels."

One of the core principles of hermeneutics — which is the science of biblical interpretation — is to reject the temptation to bring your personal presuppositions into the interpretation of a passage. Don't read anything into a section of scripture that is not already there, but instead let the actual words speak for themselves.

As we use that hermeneutical tool for unpacking this passage, we see that nothing inherent in John 15 has anything to do with whether a person is saved or not. It says nothing whatsoever about hellfire and damnation. When we simply take Jesus's words at face value, we see that He is giving some final words to His disciples, prepping them for success after He is gone.

Here we see Jesus saying, "You are branches. You belong to me. You are in me so stay close to me. Abide in me." He is not telling people how to be saved. He's not warning them of hell. He's saying, "In order to represent me after I'm gone, you need to be connected to the vine. That's how you will bear much fruit that will glorify the Father."

Remember that Jesus is using an analogy to help His

followers bear quality fruit. Nothing in the context of this the verse speaks of hell and damnation. He's saying, "You can be a child of God and still not bear fruit, so don't be like branches that are good for nothing." That's the main point of this passage.

Therefore, let's take Jesus at His word and not be good-for-nothing Christians on our way to heaven. Be good for something. Bear fruit. Do a good job of representing Jesus. Be a part of His move in the earth. Be a part of seeing His kingdom come. Don't be a good-for-nothing branch.

This is exactly what Jesus said in the Sermon on the Mount:

> *"You are the salt of the earth; but if the salt loses its flavor, how shall it be seasoned? It is then good for nothing but to be thrown out and trampled underfoot by men. You are the light of the world. A city that is set on a hill cannot be hidden. Nor do they light a lamp and put it under a basket but on a lampstand and it gives light to all who are in the house. Let your light so shine before men, that they may see your good works and glorify your Father in heaven.* — Matthew 5:13-16

Jesus is making the same point here with different analogies. Here, He uses salt and light. Nobody wants to shake a tasteless white powder on their best steak. They don't put their brightest lamp under a basket. In John 15, He uses the analogy of branches that bear no fruit. Nobody wants to plant an expensive fruit tree or vine that bears no fruit.

Jesus is not trying to scare people with talk of hell. He

is calling us to represent Him in the world. At the end of this life, we will be judged not only by whether we received Christ but by our fruit. We hope to hear the Lord say, "Well done, good and faithful servant" (Matthew 25:23). He has some rewards for those who care for "the least of these." I don't know what those rewards will be, since all of heaven in itself will be a wonderful reward. But whatever extra rewards are coming, we can anticipate those by being fruitful in this life.

One promise you can count on is that if you abide in Christ, you will bear much fruit. Jesus said it so you can believe it.

What it means to "Abide"

Now we come to an important question in this study, which is:

What does the word "abide" mean?

We saw this word seven times in four verses, and "abide" appears even more times throughout the Gospel of John. Moreover, "abiding" was one of John's main messages in the epistles he wrote, which include 1 John, 2 John and 3 John. Clearly John saw the need to constantly urge believers to abide in Christ.

So what does it mean to "abide?"

The Greek word for "abide" is *meno,* which means "to reside or remain." In our vernacular, it describes what we do in our permanent residence.

When I call my mother and the phone rings and rings
— if she doesn't pick up the phone and it goes to voicemail
— I typically call my sister and say, "Hey Gwen. Where's
Mom? She's not answering the phone."

And Gwen usually says, "It's okay. Today she got so-
and-so to take her to such-and-such."

Then I know Mama's okay. It's her permanent
residence and she doesn't go out much. So when I call and
she doesn't pick up, I'm a little concerned and I need to
know she's alright. In the natural realm, people get
connected to their permanent dwelling places.

The same principle ought to be true in the spiritual
realm. Jesus tells us to abide; to make our permanent
residence in Him. He's not looking for holiday Christians;
for weekend visitors. He doesn't call people to put on a
Christian façade and use the Bible as a prop. That's not
making Him our permanent resident. That's a temporary
affiliation with Jesus. That's not abiding in Christ.

Residents are fully invested in a place. Their name is on
the deed. They take good care of the place. They go to
neighborhood meetings. They say, "This is mine. This is
where I live."

Jesus said, "If you want to bear fruit, you have to reside
in me. If you want to be upwardly mobile in the kingdom
of God, you can't just have a loose affiliation with me.
Superficiality won't cut it. We can't just hang out every
now and then. I have to be your *life*. Your *entire life*. You
can't treat me like a vending machine, coming to me

whenever you need help, pushing the button and claiming goodies from God."

People who abide in Jesus don't just show up when it's convenient. They don't only come to Him when they need a little supernatural intervention. They don't only come to Him when they need a miracle. They don't only come to Him in times of trouble or to claim new cars and houses and blessings.

Some people take John 15:7 out of context, picking out the part that reads, "ask what you desire and it shall be done for you." Their eyes get greedy and they interpret that as an invitation to an open line of credit with God. They think that God is obligated to give them every single thing they want. They see Jesus as their magic genie.

Don't take scripture out of context. The phrase about asking and receiving comes with a prior condition, which says, "If you abide in me and my words abide in you ..." The prior condition is to abide in Jesus and allow His words to abide in you. People often make the mistake of trying to claim a promise of scripture without looking at all the conditions the promise is tied to. When people say, "Jesus says I can get whatever I desire from Him," back up and see what it says earlier. Don't sail right past the conditions.

If you abide in me and my words abide in you ...

First you have to abide in Christ. You have to be centered in Him. Only then will you know what His will for your life is. You can't just claim anything you want. You can't say, "I'm believing God for a Bentley." Why would God give you a Bentley out of the clear blue sky, just because you want one? How is that abiding in Him?

If you are abiding in Christ, you will be in tune with His higher purpose for your life. Your focus will be on the fruitfulness He wants to accomplish in you. As you abide in Christ, you will be overwhelmed with the wonderful conviction that God is so much more than a genie or a vending machine. He is Lord!

We think we know what we need from God, but He knows so much better than anyone what's best for us. Jesus said:

> *"If you then, being evil, know how to give good gifts to your children, how much more will your Father who is in heaven give good things to those who ask Him."* — Matthew 7:11

Many Christians struggle to "know how to give good gifts" to their spouse or friends or children. They also need to learn how *not* to give when it's inappropriate. A good parent won't spoil a child with every gift they want, especially if they're living in disobedience. There's something wrong with a child who refuses to take out the trash and clean up their room all year long, and then in November they bring a whole heap of *gotta-haves* on their Christmas list. If you don't get respect from that child and you buy them what they want, you will live to regret it. That kind of giving is only preparing them for jail. It teaches them that they can have whatever they want, with no expectations or responsibility attached.

Establish a work ethic and a sense of responsibility in your children. They need to learn early that everyone in a family does their part. Parents who don't give their kids jobs at home should not be surprised how helpless they will be out in the workplace. Who wants to hire folk who don't know how to clean up after themselves or take directions? They can't practice in public what they never learned at home. The best parents know how to teach responsibility and respect. They love their kids too much to give them everything they want.

Thankfully, many of us had parents who wouldn't tolerate kids who refused to give while being eager to take. They taught us respect. They knew better than to spend their hard-earned money on our list of wants. Yes, they gave us a lot of the things we asked for in the end, but only to the extent that we were fully invested in the give and take of home life.

This is what it means to abide in Jesus and to make Him your permanent residence. You will be in permanent residence when you learn to respect others, to serve others and to use your gifts and talents not only for yourself. Abiding in Christ means assimilating His will, His way and His purpose into everything you do and say. It means worshiping Him with every breath you take. When you abide in Christ, you live each moment to glorify Him. You serve His purpose every step of the way. Your values are His values. Your thoughts become His thoughts in you.

This is what it means to abide in Christ.

The Apostle Paul said:

For to me, to live is Christ and to die is gain. —
Philippians 1:21

In this first chapter of Philippians, Paul debates whether it is better to stay here on earth to keep ministering to the people who need him or to go home to be with Jesus in heaven. Paul knew that earth is not our permanent residence. He knew we are pilgrims passing through an earthly experience, traveling toward heaven, our eternal home. So even though he knows he's not in charge of the timing, Paul wonders, "Is it better to stay here or to go home?"

Again, we need to look at the context of these words in order to arrive at the proper meaning. Earlier in Philippians 1:7, Paul lets his readers know that he is imprisoned. He is in chains. And as a prisoner of the Romans, he is living with a lot of uncertainty. His life is in the hands of Caesar. At any moment he could be dragged to his execution. It wasn't like he was trying to decide which step he should take, toward life or toward death. He was simply stating the fact that this choice could be made for him at any time. He says, "I don't know whether I'm staying or whether I'm going. Personally, I would gain a lot by dying. But on the other hand, if I stay, I can be a blessing to you all. Why? Because for me to live is all about Christ. He's the only reason I'm here."

So in this passage, Paul was showing us how to make our permanent residence in Christ, even while traveling as pilgrims through this transient world.

What are You Living for?

Let's talk about your purpose. More specifically:

What are you living for?

Look to the vineyard. A healthy, functioning branch will be bearing fruit in the context of the vine. A healthy branch is not confused about its purpose. It lives to bear fruit, abiding in the life-giving vine.

If you want to be truly happy and make a positive difference in this world, examine what you're living for. Some people live for pleasure. Some live for recognition or success. Some live for prosperity. Some live for the almighty dollar. Some live for partnerships and for other people.

Whatever has become your main focus, surrender that to God's priorities so your life will be built on the right foundation. Paul said, "I consider my life worth nothing" (Acts 20:24). His relationship with Christ was more important than anything. God isn't against money or prosperity, but He *is against* prosperity being your focus. Earthly treasures cannot be your focus when you cultivate the fruit of the Spirit. Seek *first* God's kingdom (Matthew 6:33). Abide in Christ *first* and He will take care of you. Even if you're poor like I've been, abide in Christ first.

I've met plenty of folk who thought being broke gives you an exemption from giving and tithing, but that's not how I see it. I first entered vocational ministry in 1982, when the membership of my father's church had outgrown his ability to maintain a personal, hands-on approach. He wanted to know everybody's name and be involved in their lives. So he asked the leadership to pray for an assistant pastor and after a period of time, everyone came back with the same answer.

"The Lord said Paul should be your assistant pastor."

So Pops said, "All right then. My son's going to be my assistant pastor."

In truth, that created some tension because I wasn't like my father when it came to temperament. He was the ultimate people person. He was always talking and hanging out with folk, praying with them and sharing meals with them. Back in the days before cellphones, you might have thought the phone receiver was attached to his head, with that long twisty cord following him all over the house. He'd even miss family meals, calling to say he was over at so-and-so's house. "I'm at Aunt T's. I'm at the Jamaican family's house. Oh, and they got some delicious curried goat."

My father couldn't get enough of fellowshipping with other people, but I wasn't built that way. I didn't have that personality. I didn't want to be away from home all the time. I had my boundaries and I was happy seeing folk at church, but I wasn't about to leave the front door wide open all the time. So in March of 1982, the leadership convinced my dad to hire me as their first assistant pastor. Then when they considered my salary and came up with a figure, my father said, "Y'all don't have to worry about that. He doesn't need that much."

And I thought, "Wait. I'm getting married in six weeks and you're saying I don't have needs? Huh!?"

I knew the devil was in there somewhere but I wasn't sure exactly how. Still, my dad liked the idea of me starting off small, so that's what happened. I couldn't question it because although God had called me to this position, He never promised me financial security. He only said, "Your assignment is to learn shepherding under your father. You will learn what priorities you have to develop."

So under my father, I learned some things that didn't come natural to me, like empathy and sensitivity. When people shared their pain with me, I'd nod and say, "Oh, I'm so sorry." But at the time, it seemed so fake compared to my dad, who would be crying and carrying on. I had genuine compassion but the tears just didn't come. Still, I learned a lot about how to empathize under my father. He didn't change who I was, but He changed my priorities. In the years since, I learned how to be a good shepherd without changing my personality. I have even come to appreciate that Pop didn't want to advance me too soon. He knew that if I was immediately bringing home a comfortable paycheck, there were some things I'd never learn.

In other words, *seek first God's kingdom*. Put God's purpose above everything. Keep asking yourself: *What am I living for?*

Live for purpose. Seek God's kingdom first and He will add more besides. Don't criticize godly men and women who drive nice cars or live comfortably, because you might be seeing them at the wrong season. Years earlier, they might have been driving raggedy cars and scraping to get by.

You can't be trusted with more stuff if you don't know how to be faithful with a little, so get your priorities in order. Pleasure can be a great feature of life but it can't be your focus. When people say, "I wanna enjoy the best that life has to offer," that's great as a feature, but it can't be your focus.

Your focus needs to be on the will of God, so be rooted in Christ.

If you're buying pleasures you can't afford, something's wrong. If you're going on vacations you can't afford, have a good stay-cation instead. Go local instead of the Caribbean. If you're mortgaged up to your eyeballs, put God's kingdom first. Get your priorities in order. Don't overreach your ways and means. Enjoy prosperity and pleasure when it comes, but make sure your focus is on Christ.

Partnerships cannot be your main focus. Yes, partnerships are great. Marriage is a wonderful institution that is sanctioned in heaven. It's okay to ask God to bring you a great spouse, but don't think He's obligated to give you what you want. God blesses you should you find a suitable person to marry. He will sanction that marriage. When I marry couples, I expect God to bless the couple's decision, but I also expect godly men and women to make a wise decision and not rush into a commitment based on feelings and infatuation. Too many folk wake up after the honeymoon with regrets, saying, "I moved too fast. I wasn't looking for the right thing. I jumped on the first train coming down the track. I wish somebody had knocked some sense into my head."

I learned this early on, not long after going into ministry at my dad's church. The first couple I married hadn't been married more than a year when the young lady came into my office for a meeting. She sat there looking me straight in the eye and said, "Why did you let me do that? I wish I'd never married that man." It broke my heart. Naturally, we had done a bit of counseling before they got married, but mainly I was green back then. I didn't know a lot. If they came to me now, I doubt they would have made it through the pre-engagement counseling. It's important to catch folk pre-engagement, because pre-marital is often too late. It's hard to talk to folk when they're blinging. Once the invitations go out, nearly all bets are off. You can't talk sense anymore because they don't hear it. I like to catch them when they're first falling in love. Come in with goose bumps and we'll see if they're still there when I get through with you.

Couples going into marriage need love, not infatuation. What's love? That's a question we will answer when we get to the first fruit of the Spirit. In that chapter you'll become familiar with the different types of love that are described in scripture. The love that makes a marriage successful is *agape*. It's the only kind of love that can weather the storms of life. It transcends circumstances. It continues even when the one you love gets on your nerves and tries your patience.

At a certain point in everyone's marriage, the honey drips off the moon. The sweetness fades … not permanently, but for a season. Through shifting circumstances and changing emotions, you need a love that anchors. You need a love that abides even through seasons of questioning and regret.

My advice for those who are on the front end of engagement and marriage is to know what you're getting into. Don't blame God when you don't get what you want. Don't catch a train just because you're feeling desperate on the platform. If you're still waiting for the good one to come, stop waiting. The last thing a good one needs to find is a desperate, needy person waiting on the platform. Get discipled and continue conforming into the image of Christ. This applies to both women and men. We have a generation of males who know how to make babies but don't know how to raise them, who have not learned how to provide and protect.

Never believe that life is on hold until you find that certain someone. Jesus is in the business of improving lives, taking them from glory to glory. While you're waiting for someone to arrive, let Christ cultivate good fruit in your life. Jesus can change you. He can turn you around. Like the gospel song that says:

He will pick you up and turn you around.
He'll place your feet on solid ground.
Come to Jesus, right now.[3]

---

[3] "If you Come to Him," by Edwin Hawkins, from the "Worthy" album (Paradise Records, 1994).

He can do that. And as He does, don't make decisions based on desperation or wrong desires. If you are single, learn to live victoriously single. Keep your perspectives in order. Know what you are living for and stay on the right track.

What are you living for?

Live for purpose. Seek God's kingdom. Learn to abide in Christ.

Developing Godly Character: The Fruit of the Spirit

Earlier, we saw how Jesus said, "I am the vine, you are the branches. He who abides in me and I in him bears much fruit" (John 15:5). We saw how God specifically chose us and appointed us to bear fruit (John 15:16). Bearing fruit is

not an option for Christians. It is a part of our spiritual nature. It is who we are. We are the branches and Jesus is the vine. We are fruit-bearers and the fruit of the Spirit is essential for Christian character development.

In his letter to the church in Galatia, the Apostle Paul uncovered the practical applications of what Jesus taught about bearing fruit. Specifically, Paul mentioned nine character traits that are essential components of the fruit of the Spirit. Although some biblical scholars may limit the fruit of the Spirit to these nine qualities, I believe they are just a sampling of the godly virtues that Christians are called to express. In the Bible, we see a number of other positive character traits like wisdom, brotherly kindness, humility and godliness. For now, though, we will focus on the nine character traits mentioned in the book of Galatians.

Here's what the Apostle Paul wrote about the fruit of the Spirit:

But the fruit of the Spirit is love, joy, peace, longsuffering, kindness, goodness, faithfulness, gentleness and self-control. Against such there is no law. — Galatians 5:22-23

Notice how Paul describes the "fruit" of the spirit, not the "fruits" of the spirit. This makes sense when you think of grapes or berries that grow in clusters. If you want to experience the fullness of cluster fruit, you take the whole package. You don't pick and choose. In the same way, the fruit of the Spirit is a unified package deal.

Imagine how out of balance your life would be if you were full of joy but had no love or peace or goodness. You'd be grinning and laughing while hating and causing all kinds of trouble. God doesn't want you to be all joy and no love. He doesn't want you to be all longsuffering and no kindness. You'd be a mean person who could endure hardship. That's not the kind of character God wants to form. He develops character in clusters. While you're growing in love, He wants to develop joy and peace and self-control. Expect God to develop the fullness of the fruit of the Spirit in all of these nine areas and more.

Successful gardeners know that in order to bear good fruit, they need to nurture the soil and pull up the weeds and trim the vines. In a similar way, our lives need to be cultivated if we expect to nurture the fruit of the Spirit. This requires our deliberate submission to the Holy Spirit, as we yield to His pruning and cultivation.

Some people are proudly unforgiven. They'll mug you for something you did years ago, making you wonder, "Why are you still back there? Didn't we talk about forgiveness and moving on?"

The Greek word for "forgive" is *aphiemi*, which means *to send* or *to put at a distance*. To forgive an offense means to send it away; to put it at a distance. Once you repent of a sin or forgive someone, release it. Send it away. Don't hold it close. Don't keep reminding yourself of what happened.

Even if someone doesn't appear to be sorry, send it away. You don't even have to tell them that you forgive them. Your main need is to release it and refuse to live in unforgiveness. Look at Jesus on the cross. He was surrounded by folk who weren't sorry in the least for what they were doing to Him and yet He said, "Father, forgive them." He wasn't talking *to* them. He was talking to the Father *about* them. He was showing us how to untangle ourselves from unforgiveness.

This is how God develops rich character in His people. He offers us the amazing fruit of the Spirit to enrich our lives. He teaches us to prune the negative thoughts and actions and enrich the positive.

We have seen what it means to abide in the Lord and bear fruit that remains. Now let us unpack each of these nine treasures that are collectively known as the fruit of the Spirit.

Abide in the Lord and you will bear much fruit!

Love

*But the fruit of the
Spirit is **love**, joy, peace,
longsuffering, kindness,
goodness, faithfulness,
gentleness and self-control.*
— *Galatians 5:22-23*

God develops our character by offering us the amazing fruit of the Spirit to enrich our lives. He teaches us to prune negative character traits and make room for positive ones. These are some of the most important life-giving lessons from the vineyard.

In this chapter, we will study the first virtue in God's amazing cluster of fruit, which is *love*.

What is love?

Love is an extremely complex thing. It can mean so many different things to different people. We can "love" nearly *anything* these days, from our spouse and kids to the latest fast food craze.

You will absolutely <u>love</u> this bacon cheeseburger!

You might hear about a bacon cheeseburger that's "to

die for," but would you really die for a fast food meal? Do you love it as much as you love your child or your parent or your spouse? What does the word "love" even mean?

In English, you can *love* just about anything, but the same is not true in all languages. The New Testament Greek actually has four very distinct words to describe four different aspects of love. This precision of language helps to enrich our understanding of God's ultimate design for love in the lives of believers.

What follows is a brief summary of the four different words for "love" that were used by Greek-speaking people at the time of Christ.

Agape love is a divine, other-centered love. It's the love that caused Jesus to die on the cross so that we can live. It's also the love that's mentioned in Galatians 5:22: "But the fruit of the Spirit is love ..." This is how I like to define *agape* love: ***The purely motivated resolve to think and act in the other person's best interest.***

Phileo refers to friendship love. It is the love between good friends. "Philadelphia" means "the city of brotherly love," although in my experience, it might be more appropriate to call it "the city of brotherly shove." *Phileo* involves mutual support and respect and fondness.

Storge means "family love." It's rarely used in the New Testament but *storge* describes the natural affection and connectedness that family members experience toward each other. People say that "blood is thicker than water," and in the same way *storge* is strong in a functional family.

Eros is erotic love. It is the kind of romantic love that God created to be experienced in the context of marriage. It is a sexual love that is good and beautiful when used how God intended for it to be used.

So you see how the Greek language helps to clarify the unique distinctions between these different aspects of what we call "love" in English. In this study, we will dig deeper into the concept of love as found in scripture and explore its practical applications for each one of us today.

Agape Love

When Paul writes "The fruit of the Spirit is love," he uses the word *agape*.

Agape is the *purely motivated resolve to think and act in the other person's best interest.*

Agape love is "purely motivated," which means it comes from a pure place. You have no ulterior motives when you love in this way. If someone is looking to get something in return for their so-called love, it's not *agape*. *Agape* is motivated from a pure place.

Agape also has resolve. It reacts to decisions, not feelings. It is thoughtful. It is committed. This is an important aspect of love that our culture has largely missed, because people confuse love with feelings.

"I looked across the crowded room and fell in luv ..."

That's the problem. You fell. Resolve had nothing to do with it. Your feelings took control. Thoughtful decisions had nothing to do with it. You had no resolve to think and act in the other person's best interest.

If you want to know how to love, just look at the One who designed love:

> *"For God so loved the world that He gave His only begotten Son, that whoever believes in Him should not perish but have everlasting life." — John 3:16*

The Greek word used here is *agape*. "For God so *agaped* the world ..."

Who did God *agape*?

The world.

He *agape*d all of us. By His own resolve and with pure motives, God determined to think and act in our best interest. If you want to know what love is, look to Jesus. He is the best expression of love you will ever find.

Let's consider four important qualities of *agape* love.

1) Agape is Supernatural.

Agape is supernatural. That means it does not originate from a human source. You and I cannot experience *agape* unless we have God in us and allow God to convey His love through us. In other words, we are conduits of God's love.

Without God, there can be no *agape*. Without God, it is impossible to *agape* our enemies like Jesus told us to do (Matthew 5:44; Luke 6:27). Our human nature leads us to pick and choose who to love, but God's supernatural love makes it possible for us to love everybody.

In his first epistle, the Apostle John wrote:

Beloved, let us love one another, for love is of God and everyone who loves is born of God and knows God. He who does not love does not know God, for God is love. — 1 John 4:7-8

John says we should love one another because "love is of God." In the Greek, "of God" is more accurately translated "from God."

Love is from God.

You can't get love from any other source. God is the only provider. You have to get it directly from the source. This fact is underscored in verse eight where it says, "for God is love." So, love comes from God because God is love.

Don't let this distinction pass you by. God doesn't just *have* love. Anybody can *have* love, just like anybody can have a glass of water. You might have fifty gallons of water. You might even own a whole lake. You may have incredible amounts of water, but under no circumstances could you say that you "are water." What you *have* is not *who you are.*

God doesn't *have* love.
God is love.
Do you see the difference? That's who He is. His identity is love. If you're going to represent God to the

world, you have to be plugged into love. That's why Jesus said:

> *"Abide in me and I in you. As the branch cannot bear fruit of itself unless it abides in the vine, neither can you unless you abide in me. I am the vine, you are the branches. He who abides in me and I in him bears much fruit; for without me you can do nothing."* — John 15:4-5

Fruitfulness comes from being connected to the source. We receive love from God because God is love. God wants us to represent Him on earth, blessing others with the abundant fruit of the Spirit, but that can only happen when we are connected to love.

Agape love is supernatural. It is not available anywhere else. To experience *agape* love, we need to be plugged into the Source.

2) Agape is Selfless

Agape love is not only supernatural but it is selfless. To explore this point, let's look at the parable of the Prodigal Son beginning with the first two verses:

> *Jesus continued: "There was a man who had two sons. The younger one said to his father, 'Father, give me my share of the estate.' So he divided his property between them."* — Luke 15:11-12 (NIV)

Can you believe that!? This kid walks up to his daddy and says, "Gimme!" If I'd have done that with my pop, first he would have tried to figure out if I'd gone temporarily insane. And next … you don't want to know what he would have done next.

Jesus is making a point here that applies to each one of us. We all have moments when we act like that second son. We show disrespect in the way we pray sometimes. "Gimme, God." We show it in the way we react when our prayers aren't answered how we like. "I don't deserve this, God." We have more younger son in us than we care to admit.

So, the younger son says, "Gimme," and in the natural we expect the father to clobber him for being disrespectful. And yet he doesn't, which makes us wonder, "Why not? Why aren't the servants scraping this kid off the floor?"

In this parable, Jesus is giving us a picture of *agape* love. The father refused to usurp the son's free will even though he knew the son couldn't survive on his own. He didn't need to bring his son low because he knew his son could do the job better himself. The father could have punished the boy by not giving him anything or by clobbering him. He could have tried to teach his son some lessons in the school of love and wisdom, but no. In the council of his own will, this father decided to not stand in the way of his son's free will. He released this boy to enroll in the school of hard knocks. He said, "This kid is a knucklehead so I'm sending him to the school of knuckleheads and hard knocks."

Can we get real here? A lot of us are feeling holy, pretending we never did anything stupid in our whole lives. Let's get off of that cloud and admit we're a lot like that second son. We did plenty of dumb things to earn a place in the school of knuckleheads. Nobody is exempt from membership there. The staff never says, "You're too old. You know better now. Don't come back anymore." You can be in your eighties and still find yourself going back to that school.

So the father of this foolish son says, "I'm not going to punish you. I'm going to get out of your way and let you learn in the school of knuckleheads."

This is a side of love that many Christians overlook. Love doesn't always try to fix things. Sometimes love simply steps aside and lets the consequences do the teaching. It may seem as if the father enabled his son by giving him money but he didn't enable anything. He was simply saying, "Since you want nothing to do with me and nothing to do with the school of love and wisdom, I'm going to give you your part of the inheritance so you can take it to that other school." The father chose to do this because his love was centered on the boy's best interest.

Too many parents enable their kids by constantly rescuing them from the consequences of their wrongful choices. That's not love. Love sometimes steps aside and lets some difficult things happen. When I was young and a kid would land in the hospital after a shootout, hanging between life and death, I'd sometimes hear a parent say, "Thank you, Jesus. Maybe they'll listen to you now, because they sure didn't want to hear what I was trying to teach them."

Sometimes you have to step aside because that's what

love does. Here's how the story of the Prodigal Son continues:

> *"Not long after that, the younger son got together all he had, set off for a distant country and there squandered his wealth in wild living. After he had spent everything, there was a severe famine in that whole country and he began to be in need. So he went and hired himself out to a citizen of that country who sent him to his fields to feed pigs. He longed to fill his stomach with the pods that the pigs were eating, but no one gave him anything.*
>
> *"When he came to his senses, he said, 'How many of my father's hired servants have food to spare and here I am starving to death! I will set out and go back to my father and say to him: Father, I have sinned against heaven and against you. I am no longer worthy to be called your son; make me like one of your hired servants.'"* — Luke 15:13-19 (NIV)

That boy went out and lived buck wild, but when the money was gone, so were his friends. He was all alone with no money, no friends, no food. Hunger is a good teacher, so this boy was finally getting to a place where he could learn some important lessons in the school of hard knocks. He ended up hiring himself out to feed a man's pigs. Anybody hearing this story from Jesus would have said, "Pigs? This boy is a Jew. He has no business messing with pigs." It goes to show you that wrongful choices can land you in places where you ought not to go.

An enabling parent might be surprised and shocked at how far this child had fallen, but not this loving father. He stepped out of the way so his boy could learn how costly it was to attend the school of knuckleheads and hard knocks. There's no tuition higher than that school. It took that boy to a place of desperation, but that was okay with the father who knew it would bring him to his senses.

Here's what happened next:

"So he got up and went to his father. But while he was still a long way off, his father saw him and was filled with compassion for him. He ran to his son, threw his arms around him and kissed him." — Luke 15:20 (NIV)

The father could not have seen him a long way off unless he was actively watching and waiting. This tells us that the father's love never left that boy. He never gave up on his son. He continually prayed for his restoration. So while the boy was making these stupid decisions, the father was still hopeful.

That reminds me of Paul's words in 1 Corinthians 13: *[Love] bears all things, believes all things, hopes all things, endures all things.* — *1 Corinthians 13:7*

Love always hopes. It wants the right thing. Love allows bad circumstances to teach others but it doesn't rejoice in those circumstances. It's not hateful, saying, "Boy, I hope they get what they deserve." Love is looking for the other person's restoration and their best interest.

The father was looking. If we want to bless those we love, we have to keep looking. We have to keep watching and praying. As disrespectful and entitled as this boy had been, the father's selfless *agape* love hoped and prayed that he would land on his feet and find restoration.

Agape love is supernatural.
Agape love is selfless.

3) Agape is Steadfast

Agape love is steadfast.

The prodigal son's father didn't give up on him. He waited patiently with a heart full of compassion. This shows us how steadfast love doesn't say, "I'm through with you. I gave you a year. You took up too much of my time. Now, I'm done with you." *Agape* love is steadfast, never giving up.

I'm not saying that people who are abused should be steadfast and stay with the abuser. You need to get yourself out of harm's way. You shouldn't put up with that. If it's an abusive marriage, separate yourself and get to a safe place where you can decide if there are biblical grounds for divorce. But even divorce doesn't mean you stop loving. God calls us to love even those who hate us. God is like the good father in the story who never gave up on his son and we need to follow His example.

With this challenge from God's word, I can imagine some people saying, "Would you please get on to the other fruit? I heard enough about this *agape* stuff." Well, hang in there, okay? *Agape* keeps on loving even when the one you love is unresponsive, unkind, unloving and unworthy.

Agape keeps on loving even when the one you love is unresponsive, unkind, unloving and unworthy.

In the natural, you want to love folk only as long as they are responsive and kind. But the moment things go south, you're out of there. This is a fact of life in the natural world, but it's not God's way. *Agape* will keep loving even when there's no love coming back. Why?

Because God's love is steadfast.

4) Agape is Sacrificial

Agape love is supernatural.
Agape love is selfless.
Agape love is steadfast.
Agape love is sacrificial.

Let's see how the story of the Prodigal Son continues:

"And the son said to him, 'Father, I have sinned against heaven and in your sight and am no longer worthy to be called your son.' But the father said to his servants, 'Bring out the best robe and put it on him and put a ring on his hand and sandals on his feet. And bring the fatted calf here and kill it and let us eat and be merry; for this my son was dead and is alive again; he was lost and is found.' And they began to be merry."
— Luke 15:21-24 (NIV)

Can you believe it? In today's figures, this kid easily got a million dollars' worth of inheritance from his rich pop. So after burning all that, he came home and got a robe and sandals and a ring — which is like a credit card that allows him to spend his daddy's money in the marketplace. The father's love is off the charts!

All of that, of course, came after the son demonstrated a repentant attitude. He humbled himself, came back home and acknowledged his wrong. You can't give those things to people who haven't learned enough to acknowledge that they were wrong.

This boy said, "Father, I've sinned. I'm not worthy to be called your son." Verse 19 tells us that the son was planning to say even more but his father cut him short. Once his father saw the repentance, he knew it was time to reinvest. He said, "Here, take a robe. Take some sandals. Take the credit card. Kill that calf. We're going to have a *par-teee!*" For all we know, the Cupid Shuffle might have started right there in Luke 15. They're enjoying the barbeque singing, "To the left. To the left." Maybe Luke just forgot to write that part down.

When repentance has taken place, *agape* keeps no record of wrongs. Naturally, we all have a memory. We can't help but remember some things, but we shouldn't keep rehearsing all the details. What we need is a forgiving heart; a resolve to send it away; a willingness to release the other person for what they've done.

Here's an important fact to remember: When you hold someone in unforgiveness, it is worse for you than it is for them. You think you're punishing them by keeping them locked up in your heart but it's *you* who are bound up. You're like a prison warden watching over them all the time. You're not hurting them. You're hurting yourself! Find freedom and let them go. Forgive them and get on with your life.

The Bible says, "If your enemy hungers, feed him" (Romans 12:20). Nothing will change their life more than when they're expecting trouble from you and you send them Uber Eats. I'm trying to help you now. Doordash might be the last straw that breaks their anger and leads them into the Kingdom of God. Grubhub might be your best expression of *agape* love.

Phileo Love

As mentioned, the Greek language has four different words for "love." *Agape* is the other-centered godly love that is the first fruit of the Spirit. Let's look now at *phileo* love.

In 2 Peter 1, the Apostle Peter encourages us to add a number of qualities to our faith. He says:

> *But also for this very reason, giving all diligence, add to your faith virtue, to virtue knowledge, to knowledge self-control, to self-control perseverance, to perseverance godliness, to godliness brotherly kindness and to brotherly kindness love.* — 2 Peter 1:5-7

Peter is stressing that we cannot be people of faith without adding substance to our faith. We need other qualities like virtue, knowledge, self-control, perseverance, godliness, brotherly kindness and *agape* love. In this context, "brotherly kindness" is *phileo*.

Phileo means the kindness you find among close friends. Christians need to add both *agape* and *phileo* to their faith. Some people might say that the nine quality traits mentioned in Galatians 5 are the only fruit of the

Spirit, but I would include all of these qualities mentioned here in 2 Peter 1 as additional components of the fruit of the Spirit.

Peter says, "Add to your faith *friendship love*," or *phileo*.

Phileo love is platonic. It is rooted in mutual respect and support for one another. It has nothing to do with sexual attraction or romance, but it can be intimate. That might be difficult to understand, since we live in such a sexually-charged world. Intimacy and sex are not the same thing. You can have an intimate friendship that knits you together, but that has nothing to do with sex or romance. We shouldn't confuse *phileo* with *eros* love.

Here's an example of *phileo* love from the words of Jesus:

"Greater love has no one than this, than to lay down one's life for his friends." — John 15:13

That's *phileo* love, the kind of brotherly and sisterly love that we ought to have for each other. You need a lot of love to lay down your life for a friend, to take the bullet for them. Everybody ought to have friends like that. This is the kind of relationship that will get you through the crises of life. But not every friendship is like that. If it came down to one of your regular friends dying, you'd be playing a game of rock, paper, scissors. If you'd lose, you'd be begging for two out of three.

Jesus is not saying you'll have that kind of relationship with anybody. He is telling you it is definitely possible with some. In today's world, men especially don't have enough relationships that are intimate and platonic. God made us to be connected even when it's not a sexual thing. That's why we need *phileo* love.

When Jesus' good friend Lazarus was dying, a messenger came and told Him:

"Lord, behold, he whom you love is sick." — John 11:3

That's the word *phileo*. They were saying that his friend Lazarus — the one He loved like a brother — was sick. They didn't say he was the one Jesus *agape*d, because Jesus *agape*d the whole world. This was a special friend with whom He had an intimate, platonic relationship.

To have a fulfilled life, you need more than God's *agape* love for everybody. You need to have *phileo* love for some. You may have hundreds or thousands of acquaintances, but only a few that you call sister or brother. If you don't have anyone like that in your life, begin looking for them today.

The Bible tells us about many more *phileo* friendships, including the one between Jonathan and David.

Now when he had finished speaking to Saul, the soul of Jonathan was knit to the soul of David and Jonathan loved him as his own soul. — 1 Samuel 18:1

A lot of people in our sexually-charged culture are likely to think that's talking about something more than platonic friendship, but it's not. In the Jewish context, it was common to have intimate friendships that had nothing to do with *eros*. This is how life is supposed to be.

There are other purpose-driven partnerships in the Bible, like that between Aaron and Moses, who were not only friends but blood brothers (Exodus 6:20). When Moses' stuttering problem got in the way, Aaron stepped in and said, "I'll be your spokesman. You tell me what to say."

In Ruth 1, we read about the covenant relationship between Naomi and Ruth. They were not related by blood but by marriage. When their husbands died, Naomi told her daughters-in-law Ruth and Orpah, "I'm going back to Bethlehem, my hometown. You all aren't from there. You stay here in Moab, your country. Maybe you'll find men to marry here."

Orpah gave it some thought and said, "You're right, Naomi. Give me a kiss and a hug. Stay in touch, okay? Bye."

Notice how Naomi didn't put a guilt trip on Orpah and shame her into coming along, which is a lesson in itself. Don't try to drag your Orpahs into seasons they ought not to be in. Give them your love and your blessing. Pray for them and be willing to welcome them with open arms if they ever come calling.

On the other hand, Ruth was stuck like glue to Naomi. "Your God will be my God," she said. "Your people will be my people. Where you live, I will live. Where you die, I will die. We'll hang together for the rest of our lives." God knit these women together and it was purpose-driven because Ruth went on to marry a man named Boaz from Bethlehem and they both became the ancestors of Jesus Christ.

God has an important purpose for the relationships in your life. You won't be able to get to the places He wants you to go without some *phileo* friends, so cultivate these relationships in your life.

In 1 Kings 19, we read how the Prophet Elijah chose Elisha to be his successor. This is another important type of *phileo* friendship. When you mentor someone, they will go farther into the next generation than you are able to go alone. They need you to pour into them everything you know so they can pass it on. I'm glad that my dad poured into me so I was able to go farther than he was. But I never felt as if I was greater than my dad. I knew whose shoulders I was standing on. He was a tremendous discipler of people and he put the best of that into me.

Never stop honoring those who helped get you where you are today. Don't act like you're better just because you think you accomplished more than they did. Never look across at people you need to look up to. Because of them, you are where you are, so never forget that.

Four Basics of True Phileo Friendship

I'd like to take a moment to highlight four important points that will help explain the basics of *phileo* love and friendships.

1) Be Appropriately Friendly to Everyone, but not Everyone is a True Friend

There is a big difference between *friendliness* and *friendship*. We don't have to be everybody's true friend but we do need to be appropriately friendly to everyone. We need to be polite and kind to people we don't know, even to enemies. The world makes it extremely easy to be non-relational toward practically everybody, but we have to cut that out. The Bible tells us to personally engage people. How can we win people if we won't engage them?

I know this will go against some people's nature, but *get used to being nice.* Do something radically crazy in your neighborhood and *go out of your way to talk to people.* There are unspoken rules in neighborhoods that tell you to mind your own business. Well, break the rules!

I recently did that with a neighbor who's never spoken to me in all the years I've lived in this neighborhood. I said, "Howdy" and he actually spoke back to me! I broke the taboo. I was kind to him and he was kind back to me.

Shock some people on the elevator by smiling right into their faces and saying, "Hello! Hope you're having a good day." People might think that's crazy but it's not. What's crazy is how folk can be cramped up within two feet of each other, day after day, and pretend that the other person doesn't exist. Everybody's looking at the changing numbers, not saying a word.

Friendliness is always appropriate, but don't consider everybody to be a true friend.

Here are three things to know about true friends:

First, a true friend loves at all times (Proverbs 7:17).

That means your acquaintances who don't love you consistently aren't your true friends. They're your fair weather friends. They're the ones who like to be around you when it's convenient or when they get something in return.

Second, true friends wound to heal. Proverbs says:

Faithful are the wounds of a friend, but the kisses of an enemy are deceitful. — Proverbs 27:6

Like a good doctor, true friends cut to heal, not to kill. It's the "frenemies" who only want to cut you down. You can be appropriately friendly around them, but watch your back side because they will never be your true friend. When a faithful friend says things that hurt, they'll do it with *phileo* love. They'll give you some anesthesia first to help you take the pain. You know they're about to bring out the scalpel when they say, "You know I love you, right?" That's the anesthesia because they're getting ready to cut you.

You can trust a faithful friend who cuts you with love. They won't humiliate you. They'll never dress you down in front of others. When you are vulnerable, a friend will scoop you up and take you to a private place of triage and safety.

Third, true friends are faithful in all different seasons. We need friends who will take care of us when we're at our worst. We need friends to celebrate our successes. We need friends to laugh with us when we are happy and cry with us when we're sad. I get texts and calls from friends like these asking for prayer, announcing some great event or just to say, "Hey. How are you doing?" True friends are faithful in all different seasons.

2) Be Intentional about Cultivating Strong Friendships

We are talking about some of the basics of true friendship. The first basic is:

Be appropriately friendly to everyone, but not everyone is a true friend.

The second thing to know is this:

Be intentional about cultivating strong friendships.

If you need strong friendships, prayer is a good place to start, but don't finish there. It's no wonder your prayers aren't being answered if all you do is pray "God, give me friends" while never reaching out to anyone. God has already put people in your sphere of influence. If you're Ruth, Naomi is already there. If you're Elisha, Elijah is already there. If you're Jonathan, David is already there. You just need to develop those friendships. If you're not sure if they'll pass the test, then vet them first. Get together with them and check it out. See if this is somebody you can build a trusting relationship with. If they're so full of themselves that they can't stop talking about themselves, you'll know they're not a true friend long before dessert arrives.

Be intentional about cultivating strong relationships with the right people.

3) Singles, Be Intentional about Enjoying Life as a Single

These last two points are specifically for singles.

Singles, be intentional about enjoying life as a single.

While you're single, enjoy your life on purpose as a single. Don't major in being a marriage wannabe. If you're complaining about not having anybody to take you on a cruise, sister, then get your girlfriends to go with you. Enjoy life intentionally. Quit sitting around wanting things you don't have. Work with what you have.

Develop qualities that are attractive on a deeper, more eternal level. Folk aren't attracted to someone who's sitting by the side of the road waiting for a hero to scoop them up on a white horse. They aren't attracted to needy people always looking for life to happen to them. Make life happen! Be happy with who you are right now and get the best out of life just the way things are. Then when that special someone comes along, you will be healthy, happy and attractive, with plenty of strengths to pour into that new relationship.

4) Be both Kind and Clear with the People you Date

Singles, be both kind and clear with the people you date. There's no sense in playing games. If all you want is a movie and a meal, make that known up front. Be very clear before that first date. Say, "I just need you to know that I'm not looking for a spouse but I'd love to go out to a movie together. If you use hand sanitizer, you can even share my popcorn. Or get your own popcorn. Whatever you prefer is fine."

As a brother or sister who is building *phileo* and *agape*, you need to be kind and clear. Respect the people you date. Don't mistreat them and certainly don't put your hands where they have no business going.

In closing, *phileo* is a healthy, intimate, friendship love. Seek *phileo* friends so you will be surrounded by folk who know how to nurture the fruit of the Spirit in your life.

Storge Love

In the Greek language, *storge* is the natural affection or connectedness that you feel toward relatives in a functional family. It happens naturally. It's a dutiful commitment to each other. The word *storge* rarely appears in the New Testament. If you're in a healthy, functional family, the natural connectedness of *storge* love happens spontaneously.

An unfortunate fact of life is that without a functional family, many people never get the chance to experience *storge* love. That's okay, though, because *agape* and *phileo* can compensate for that. If you have it, thank God. But if all you can do is roll your eyes and bite your tongue at family gathering, then thank God too. Either way, make significant investments into your intimate platonic relationships.

I am one of those who would definitely take a bullet for my wife and kids. Nobody bad is getting to them if I'm around. That kind of determination is driven by *storge* love. When God created the world, He embedded this natural kind of love between relatives in functional family relationships.

In his letter to the Romans, Paul uses two of these Greek words for love in the same sentence:

Be kindly affectionate to one another with brotherly love ... — Romans 12:10

Paul is saying that as believers, our love for each other should be even deeper than *phileo*. We should also practice *storge* love because we are in the same spiritual family. Our intimate platonic relationships should be bound together as if by blood. No matter how dysfunctional our natural families might be, we are in a spiritual family that ought to be functional.

As a pastor, I do all I can to promote unity and harmony among the saints because I know the immeasurable value of a functional church. We need to be functional to thrive and survive. When you have a problem with someone, go to that person and work things out. Talk *to* the person, not *about* the person.

The Bible explains how to resolve conflict and address issues in love. If you have a problem with someone, go to them alone and work it out (Matthew 18:15). If necessary, get help from an objective third party, perhaps your pastor or a counselor. Practice *storge* because we're all in the same spiritual family.

I need to stress that all of these friendship and family relationships ought to exist in tandem with *agape* love. No matter what kind of family or friendships you have, practice *agape* love, which treats people with the same compassion and respect that God has for them.

Eros Love

The fourth type of love distinguished in the Greek language is *eros*. *Eros* is the passionate, erotic love that fills the pages of romance novels. It's also seen in various relationships throughout the Bible. One prominent example is the love Jacob had for Rachel:

> *So Jacob served seven years for Rachel, and they seemed only a few days to him because of the love he had for her.* — Genesis 29:20

Eros is a great feature in marriage. And let's be honest; it helps a lot when it comes to procreation. Many a child has been conceived during some romantic evening!

It's important to know that *eros* is rooted in the emotions. It's fueled by infatuation, idealism and fantasies.

Eros affects how you feel emotionally, psychologically and physically. It kinda makes your spine quiver and your liver shiver! *Eros* is that infatuation you feel when you see that magical somebody and can't help but say, "Mmm! I like what I see."

Eros is not sinful as long as you rein it in and don't allow it to take you to a sinful place. It's a natural attraction. When you feel those feelings, the first question is, "Do I have any business acting on this natural attraction or do I need to throw some ice water on these emotions?"

The natural attraction isn't the problem, but what you

do with those feelings might become a problem. You know you're in trouble when your emotions get into the driver's seat of the car. When you let your feelings grab the steering wheel, you'll find yourself in places you never ought to go. God's word is clear about the boundaries for sex and romance, but *eros* is happy to bust through the borders. When *eros* grabs the steering wheel, you need to put it in its place and make some godly decisions based on what is good and right. *Eros* is not sinful, as long as you keep it in the right context. This is difficult advice to follow when so many romantic flicks and love songs are telling you to "follow your heart."

As the primary organist and keyboardist in my home church in Philadelphia, I often played for wedding ceremonies when church members got married. In those days, I performed and sometimes sang some really beautiful love songs, including one by Luther Vandross titled <u>So Amazing</u>:

> *Love has truly been good to me;*
> *Not even one sad day or minute have I had since you've come my way.*
> *I hope you know I'd gladly go;*
> *Anywhere you take me, it's so amazing to be loved.*
> *I'd follow you to the moon in the sky above ...*
> *'Cause we've got amazing love.*[4]

As I'd play such romantic tunes, it wasn't uncommon to look around and see couples cuddling and smiling during the ceremony. That's eros, and many married couples

---

[4] "So Amazing," by Luther Vandross, from "Give Me the Reason" album (Sony Music, 1986).

would do well to relearn and relive a little of the romance we enjoyed in years gone by!

On the other hand, single people who feel romantic toward someone must be careful to govern *eros* and not let *eros* govern them. Singles, please listen to me. If you let *eros* drive, it could easily drive you right over a cliff. So whatever you do, please don't let *eros* into the driver's seat of your life!

To review what we've learned, *agape* is a godly, other-centered love.

Phileo is a platonic, intimate, friendship love.

Storge is a natural, dutiful, family love.

Eros is a romantic, sensual love.

These types of love are distinct, but they do overlap. God calls us to undergird all our relationships with *agape; the purely motivated resolve to think and act in the other person's best interest.* It's a supernatural love from the God who *is love.* To grow in *agape,* we need to be connected to the Vine, Jesus Christ.

Abide in the Lord and you will bear much fruit!

Joy

*But the fruit of the Spirit is love, **joy**, peace, longsuffering, kindness, goodness, faithfulness, gentleness and self-control.*
— Galatians 5:22-23

Think back on a time when life was so difficult you didn't want to get out of bed in the morning. You dragged yourself through the day, barely able to hope for anything better. If this kind of joyless life ever happens to you, know that God has given you the tools to make it better. My prayer for you is that the Lord will do a work in your life, allowing you to experience the joy He gives as a fruit of the Spirit.

What kind of joy is this?

Here's a working definition for joy: ***gladness that doesn't require positive circumstances***.

The key word is "circumstances." We have been programmed to believe our attitude is dependent upon circumstances but it's not. The fruit of joy is much more abiding than superficial happiness. Happiness depends on what happens. If good things happen, it's easy to be happy. Since happiness depends on circumstances, it's transient. It can change in a heartbeat when uncomfortable situations arise.

But not joy. Joy is a character trait that can remain active in your life even when you're up against negative challenges. When things are not going your way, you can still have joy. This powerful fruit of the Spirit can lift you up and carry you past the opposition that comes against you.

To be clear, everybody experiences sadness. Even if your life is abounding with the fruit of joy, you will still have moments of sadness. We talked earlier about the need to be honest and not pretend that circumstances are better than they really are. The same principle applies here. I've heard "super-spiritual" people say that if you are a Christian, God will make sure you are never sad and never grieving. There's a Greek word for that: *bologna!* It's not helpful to pretend that hardship doesn't impact believers. God never promised us lives with no grief or sadness. When bad things happen, we get sad. It's a natural part of life. In the face of loss and separation, we *ought* to be sad. We ought to grieve when family and friends go home to be with the Lord.

Although moments of sadness cannot be avoided, we should not allow this state to define us. We need to see these moments as temporary stops on our journey through life.

Maybe you know people who are usually down and

whose character is defined by sadness. They perpetually exist in this place of darkness. When something good happens, they still gravitate toward sadness somewhere.

God does not want us to be characterized by sadness. His plan is for us to be characterized by the fruit of joy. He gave us a joy that remains. That's what we learn from John 15:

"If you keep my commandments, you will abide in my love, just as I have kept my Father's commandments and abide in His love. These things I have spoken to you, that my joy may remain in you and that your joy may be full." — John 15:10-11

When Jesus says, "These things I have spoken to you," He's talking about all the instructions He's been sharing with His disciples on the night before He was betrayed. He's saying, "Do you know why I'm saying all of this? So that my joy may remain in you and so your joy may be full."

All of this was in preparation for Jesus leaving the earth. He knew He would soon be crucified, resurrected, spend 40 days with His disciples and then ascend to the Father. With that understanding, He said, "I want to make sure you all are taken care of, so one of the things I'll leave you is my joy."

Here's a question for believers who are overcome with darkness and depression: If Jesus left you joy, why aren't you living in it? If you're not experiencing joy, then it must be an unclaimed blessing. Don't leave this blessing of joy unclaimed! Go and pick it up. The last thing you want is to leave your unclaimed freight sitting around.

Here's an interesting fact: At the time I am writing this, California is holding 9.3 billion dollars' worth of unclaimed property. This is property owned by individuals who have neglected or forgotten to pick up or claim their belongings. It includes bank accounts, stocks and bonds, un-cashed checks and unclaimed insurance benefits.[5]

That's a lot of unclaimed stuff ... so much that it's hard to imagine! It all belongs to people who would love to get access to it if they knew it was there.

The same thing happens in the spiritual realm. God has given many gifts that people neglect to receive. One of these gifts is joy. This is a valuable gift! Remember that joy is even more valuable than happiness. Happiness depends on what happens, but joy remains despite the circumstances. Joy endures because it depends on personal connectedness with the divine. We see this in John 15 where Jesus said, "I am the vine and you are the branches. So abide in me and you will bear much fruit."

Joy is a fruit of the Spirit, right? Well here's the promise: If you abide in Jesus, you have every right to be a joy-filled person. You can live a life filled with joy. Again, this doesn't mean there won't be moments of sadness, but you can have sadness and joy at the same time. You can have peace and longsuffering and every fruit of the Spirit

---

[5] "Missing Money? California Controller Is Holding $9.3B in Unclaimed Property," NBC Bay Area, February 5, 2021, www.nbcbayarea.com/news/california/missing-money-california-controller-is-holding-9-3b-in-unclaimed-property/2460114/.

during seasons of sadness and testing, because the fruit of the Spirit is not dependent on circumstances. Joy is a choice, so decide to live in joy.

In the next few sections, we will take a deeper look at happiness. There's nothing wrong with happiness, although as mentioned earlier, happiness is more superficial than joy. When you can be happy, enjoy it. Cultivate as much happiness as possible. Why? Because as we shall see, there are many tangible benefits of happiness.

Five Benefits of Happiness

Take a moment to consider these five benefits of happiness:

First, happiness makes you look and feel better. It literally helps you with your looks. Think of the sad folk you know. The sadness in their countenance diminishes their beauty. Even attractive people can ruin their looks with sour expressions. Thankfully, the contrary is true: Anyone can look beautiful if they radiate happiness. You look better when you're happy and you even feel better too.

Second, happiness has medical benefits.[6] Happiness boosts your immune system. It helps you avoid catching colds. Bad attitudes contribute to bad health, whereas a positive, happy attitude helps you fend off sickness. There are no guarantees, but happiness can boost your immune

---

[6] "How being Happier Makes you Healthier," by Daisy Coyle, Healthline.com, August 27, 2017, www.healthline.com/nutrition/happiness-and-health#TOC_TITLE_HDR_6.

system. I have seen this principle at work with people who were fighting serious illnesses. When trouble comes, don't sit around with your sad self, wallowing in pity. Get some happiness. Find those pockets of happiness and let them help you fight your battles.

Third, happiness helps reduce stress. Doctors know how stress kills. One of the best prescriptions for fighting stress is to cultivate happiness. Treat stress like an enemy, not like a welcome guest. Don't let yourself be okay with being stressed out. Find out what's stressing you and deal with it effectively. If people are stressing you out, then tell them, "This is where you need to get off of my bus. This is your stop. Please get off in the name of Jesus because you are stressing me out." Do that in love, knowing that Jesus still loves them and died for them and is pursuing them. Your job is not to try and fix them while they are dragging you down. They may be appointed by the enemy to stress you out and to mess with you, so have the grace to pull that bus over, open the door and say, "Get out." That might not sound Christian to you, but it is.

Fourth, happiness helps lower the risk of high blood pressure and heart disease. Medical studies have proven this to be true.[7] Happiness helps lower the risk of high blood pressure that leads to heart disease. If you want to live the best life you can and extend your days to serve God more effectively, then stay connected to the vine so you can have the happiness and the deeper joy that Jesus wants to give you.

---

[7] Ibid.

Finally, doctors believe that happiness may actually lengthen your life.[8] Some indicators seem to show that people who are happy live longer than those who are sad and who carry bad attitudes. Obviously, there are no promises here. Some grouchy old folk appear to be anointed with the gift of meanness. God in His wisdom sees fit to bless us with folk like this long into the latter years of life, despite our secret wishes otherwise. The important thing to know is that you can choose happiness and joy and make other people's lives happier while extending your own.

Seven Keys to Increasing your Happiness

How do you create a happier life for yourself? These seven keys will help you increase your happiness.

First, regularly express gratitude to God and others. Being grateful is a tangible way to increase your happiness quotient. What's more, be expressive with your thanks. Don't just think it. Say it. Express your gratitude to the Lord on a regular basis. Say, "I am so grateful to you for all that you do for me, past, present and future. I am grateful for everything, even when things don't go the way I want." Make a conscious decision to live permanently on the grateful side of life.

This may take some deliberate effort on your part to retrain habits of ungratefulness. Teach yourself to be thankful and grateful every moment of the day. Teach yourself when you're in the shower, giving praise and

---

[8] Ibid.

thanks to God for everything — even the challenges — in your life. As the water is washing you clean, let the Holy Spirit clear out negativity. Say, "Thank you, Lord. Thank you for waking me up this morning and starting me on my way. This is the day that the Lord has made. I will rejoice and be glad in it."

Don't be the kind of child that only comes to your Heavenly Father when you need a favor. Come to Him continually with praise and thanksgiving. When Jesus healed ten lepers, only one of them came back to express his gratitude (Luke 17). Be like that leper. Come to Jesus saying, "I just came to give you thanks. When I could not help myself, you helped me. When I was down and out, you lifted me up and brought me in. You are the one who is helping me right now. If it were not for you, Lord, there's no telling where I would be."

That's the first key to happiness: Express gratitude.

Second, be active. If you want to be happy, stay active. Don't be passive. Don't wait for opportunities to come and find you. Go out and get them. Don't just sit around with your bags packed, waiting for Jesus to come and get you. When Jesus left this earth, He gave us work to do. He told us to bear fruit. Part of bearing fruit is having good character, but part is also doing good works. Too many Christians sit around waiting for circumstances to get better, waiting for money to come, for friends to come, for that breakthrough to magically arrive. There's no faster road to despair than sitting around and feeling pity, waiting for life to improve. Don't be so pitiful. Go help somebody.

That will put a smile on your face.

If you're saying, "I wish somebody would help me," you have it turned around. You receive help by first helping others. You find friends by being friendly, so get busy. Be active. Give somebody a hand. What kind of person do you want to be? To answer that question, know that there are only three kinds of people: There are people who make things happen, people who watch things happen, and there are people who ask, "What happened?" Don't be one of the "What happened?" crew. Don't be one of the lookers.

If you find yourself watching things happen, watch long enough to get inspired. Then step out with the assurance that God has gifted you in ways that can make a difference in the lives of others. Make things happen.

That's the second key to happiness: Be active.

Third, prioritize rest. Notice I didn't say "Get rest." It's more than that. Make it an ongoing priority. Don't let rest sneak up on you when you're not paying attention. Don't be surprised when you sleep all night. Don't be proud that you get by on less sleep than others. Make good rest a priority. Living tired is a negative factor that will take a heavy toll on your happiness. Your body was made to rest.

The Bible says, "God gives his beloved sleep" (Psalm 127:2). You need good quality sleep. You need to shut off your mind, shut off your access to people and get good rest. Don't give people access to you 24/7. Use the "Do not disturb" feature on your phone. Identify those one or two people who can call you anytime in the event of an emergency. All the others won't be able to get through. Don't let yourself get woken up by their ringing at two in the morning. During the day, if you see their name on the caller I.D., you don't have to answer it. Let them go into voicemail. Don't record a dishonest message saying you're not home when you are. My landline message says, "This is the Sheppard's residence. Please leave your name, phone number and a message. Thank you and God bless you." *Beep*. Don't tell people you're not available. Why? Because sometimes you're available but you don't want to talk to them! There's nothing un-Christian about that. It's all a matter of protecting your boundaries.

In the chapter on love, we talked about *phileo* friendships — those special friends who take priority in your life and who have special access. Jesus had those kinds of friends. Lazarus was one of them. In John 11:3, some people told Jesus: "The one you love is sick." Lazarus was in Jesus' *favorites* list on his iPhone. We see the same special status with Peter, James and John. All of the disciples followed Jesus around, but at certain times — like when Jesus went to pray in the Garden of Gethsemane, as well as on the Mount of Transfiguration — He told the other disciples to hold back while He invited these special three to stay by His side.

Love all people, but only give special access to some of them. These kinds of boundaries are important for preserving the rest and the sanity you need. You know how some raggedy folk can drain the life out of you. Literally. Then when you die of exhaustion and stress, they'll have the nerve to cry at your funeral. That might sound overdramatic to you but I've seen it happen. I've seen parents run ragged by grown kids who are draining the life out of them. They're worried to death that those kids won't be able to survive without them. Then the first chance those kids have to stand on their own two feet is after the parents are dead and gone. Give them the chance now. Prioritize your rest and don't give them 24/7 access to you.

That's the third key to happiness: Prioritize rest.

The fourth way to increase your happiness is to eat to live, rather than live to eat. Let's be real, okay? There's no future in fronting. It's a struggle to cultivate good eating habits. We make that a priority so we can live to retirement age and so we won't be too sick to enjoy it. Of course sickness will happen sometimes but don't use that as an excuse to make it worse. So many of the common problems are preventable these days.

Follow the healthy recommendations of your doctor whose job it is to help you live long and well. For some people like me, it's not easy to learn to eat well when we are still breaking lifelong habits. Let's be real. I have struggled and I'm guessing that you have too. I'm not the only one with this testimony. I hope you are brave enough to say, "Yeah, pastor. I know what you're talking about. I've been living to eat but I'm ready to turn that around."

You don't have to be the kind of person who only eats grass and birdseed. I have friends like that, but that's not me. I told my doctor, "I'm not the kind of guy who will permanently give up all my pleasure stuff. So tell me something: Is it possible for me to get to where you say I need to be in my health, while occasionally dabbling in sweets."

He said, "Absolutely. As long as it's in moderation."

"Now we can talk," I said.

Every now and then I need a slice of cake. Every now and then I want a tasty treat that has little or no health value. But my doctor said, "You can have it occasionally. You just can't have it all the time."

Put food in its place. Make healthy food the centerpiece of your diet and move the other stuff to the fringes.

That's the fourth key to happiness: Eat to live.

The fifth key is to spend time outdoors. We were not made to sit in a house or an office all day long. There's a beautiful world out there. There's sunlight that will give you vitamins. When God said "Let there be light," it was a lot more glorious than the artificial lights you see indoors. The indoor lights don't give you vitamins. God created all of outdoors to bless us in a way that's just not possible indoors. Get outdoors and breathe the air. Get some physical exercise. Make it a point to get away from that screen. If your job involves sitting indoors all day long, be intentional about getting away. Schedule outdoor activities. Walk to the park or drive somewhere nice if you don't live in a walking neighborhood. Get in touch with the great outdoors because it will bless your life.

The sixth key to happiness is to cultivate a personal support system. You need a circle of friends who can lift you up, not bring you down. You need fillers to help you deal with your drainers. Drainers are people and situations that drain your energy. Like leeches, they suck the positivity out of you, leaving you with a sense of unhappiness.

In fact, you are supposed to have drainers in your life. God has gifted you to help them, to minister to them, to unload your resources into them, to make their lives better. You'll never be impactful if you don't have any drainers in your life. But maintain healthy boundaries and have a safe place to personally recharge. You need a healthy personal support system.

To a certain extent, parents are supposed to be drained by your kids. That's your God-ordained purpose — to a certain extent. You're supposed to place things in them that will help them deal with the vicissitudes of life. That's your job, but don't let it get out of balance. Parents need fillers to lift them up and encourage them. You can't live an effective life if you're only getting drained. You need a personal support system to fill you up.

That's the sixth key to happiness: Cultivate a personal support system.

The seventh key is to create appropriate boundaries. We've touched upon this concept in the previous points. When you are giving out more than you are taking in, something will eventually break. It's like a bank account. You can't have withdrawals with no deposits. Sooner or later you need to fill it back up again or it will crash.

Protect yourself by creating appropriate boundaries. Without limits, it will be impossible for you to keep doing what the Lord has appointed you to do. If people are taking and taking all the time, you have to decide when enough is enough. Make this an intentional decision … before anger and frustration and resentment set in. This is especially true in your home life. Let everyone know your new rules that include all seven keys to increasing happiness. Prioritize rest and healthy habits. Make your boundaries clear. Establish your limits.

Tell the takers in your life, "There are some things I will no longer be able to do for you. I'm not a superhero. I'm human and I have limits. You can't keep tapping into me without boundaries. I'm not your financial ATM. I'm not your emotional ATM. I can help you to an extent, but sometimes you will need to go somewhere else for help. If you don't have anybody else, go to Jesus. Go to the pastor. I'm sorry, but I can't do everything for you."

Your personal happiness depends upon knowing when to *not* allow certain people to cross your boundaries. Create appropriate boundaries. Create margins in your life. You can't live on the edge all the time. Look at a book. It has margins. Printers don't put words all the way to the dead end of the paper. If you saw a page without margins, you'd be visually overwhelmed. You need margins. You are built to have margins in your life. And if you don't have any, create boundaries in your life today.

The seven keys to increasing your happiness are:

- Express gratitude,

- Be active,
- Prioritize rest,
- Eat to live,
- Spend time outdoors,
- Cultivate a personal support system and
- Create appropriate boundaries.

When Happiness Fails, Joy Prevails

We have been looking at some very practical ways to maximize happiness in your life. Unfortunately — as we know from the human experience — hardship and tragedy happen to good and bad people alike. As diligent as we are in cultivating happiness, there are times when challenging circumstances threaten to rob us of every good feeling and leave us sour.

That's what joy is for.
Joy is not a feeling.
Joy is a promise.
Joy is a fruit of the Spirit.

While happiness depends upon circumstances, not so with joy. You have the assurance of two important aspects of joy: First, you have the assurance of possessing joy even when all the outward evidence tells you that joy is the last thing you should be experiencing. Maybe you have unfulfilled expectations. Maybe you are expecting something good but it's just not happening. Maybe you have an unfulfilled promise from God. This inner assurance is devoid of external evidence. You can see no signs of God's promise being fulfilled. You feel alone and abandoned.

If that sounds familiar, be encouraged by the story of the young virgin Mary who was visited by the angel Gabriel.

In the sixth month of Elizabeth's pregnancy, God sent the angel Gabriel to Nazareth, a town in Galilee, to a virgin pledged to be married to a man named Joseph, a descendant of David. The virgin's name was Mary. The angel went to her and said, "Greetings, you who are highly favored! The Lord is with you."

Mary was greatly troubled at his words and wondered what kind of greeting this might be. But the angel said to her, "Do not be afraid, Mary; you have found favor with God. You will conceive and give birth to a son and you are to call him Jesus. He will be great and will be called the Son of the Most High. The Lord God will give Him the throne of His father David and He will reign over Jacob's descendants forever; His kingdom will never end."

"How will this be," Mary asked the angel, "since I am a virgin?"

The angel answered, "The Holy Spirit will come on you and the power of the Most High will overshadow you. So the holy one to be born will be called the Son of God. Even Elizabeth your relative is going to have a child in her old age and she who was said to be unable to conceive is in her sixth month. For no word from God will ever fail."

"I am the Lord's servant," Mary answered. "May your word to me be fulfilled." Then the angel left her. At that time Mary got ready and hurried to a town in the hill country of Judea where she entered Zechariah's

home and greeted Elizabeth. When Elizabeth heard Mary's greeting, the baby leaped in her womb and Elizabeth was filled with the Holy Spirit. In a loud voice she exclaimed: "Blessed are you among women and blessed is the child you will bear! But why am I so favored, that the mother of my Lord should come to me? As soon as the sound of your greeting reached my ears, the baby in my womb leaped for joy. Blessed is she who has believed that the Lord would fulfill His promises to her!"

And Mary said, "My soul glorifies the Lord and my spirit rejoices in God my Savior, for He has been mindful of the humble state of His servant. From now on all generations will call me blessed for the Mighty One has done great things for me. Holy is His name. — Luke 1:26-49 (NIV)

I love how the angel said to Mary, "Greetings, you who are highly favored!" Then he tells her that she will give birth to the son of God. She is shocked but she is willing. So she asks, "How can I get pregnant? I'm a virgin."

She was engaged to Joseph. They had not had the marriage ceremony or consummated their marriage, so she wondered how this could possibly happen. Gabriel explained that the Holy Spirit would miraculously make it happen.

Skip ahead to when Mary goes to her cousin Elizabeth's house. Both Mary and Elizabeth had been visited by God's angel and both had promises from God. Elizabeth's promise was that she and Zechariah would parent John the Baptist.

There's a lesson here that we don't want to miss, as we see Mary go straight to Elizabeth's house. The lesson is this: When you have a promise from God but that promise is not yet showing, find somebody who's more pregnant with a promise than you are. Mary was barely pregnant at this point but Elizabeth was six months into her pregnancy. If you are troubled with doubt — if you can't explain the unexplainable — spend more time with those who are pregnant with promises. If you don't see external evidence of God's promises coming to pass, look to those who are manifesting His promises moment by moment. Spend more time with people of faith and your own faith will be strengthened.

Mary says, "My soul glorifies the Lord and my spirit rejoices in God my Savior." Mary's circumstances were troubling. She was likely to be accused of adultery. Matthew says that Joseph wanted to quietly end their plans to marry, until the angel of the Lord told him not to do that. Mary was undoubtedly facing a lot of stress and uncertainty and yet she chose to rise above her circumstances. She said, "My spirit rejoices in God my Savior."

Know that at times it will be impossible to rejoice in circumstances but you can always rejoice in God. The root word of "rejoice" is *joy*. Joy is a choice. Joy allows you to rejoice in God. If you can't rejoice at what's happening in your life, then rejoice in the One you are connected to. He stays closer than a brother (Proverbs 18:24). Know that God will never leave you nor forsake you (Hebrews 13:5).

Learn to find joy despite all the circumstantial

evidence. Trust that He always fulfills His promises. This underscores the first of two important aspects of joy, which is the assurance of joy even when all the outward evidence tells you that there should be no joy.

The second assurance is that we can have joy even when going through severe trials. We see this principle firmly established in the story of Paul and Silas at Philippi (Acts 16). Here they got in a lot of trouble with the local businessmen for casting a demon out of a female slave who could tell people's fortunes. These men were making a lot of money off this young woman and in their eyes, Paul and Silas had robbed them of a fortune by delivering her from the evil spirit. To say that the people were mad at Paul and Silas would be an understatement.

After the two Apostles were seized and dragged into the marketplace, here's how the story continued:

The crowd joined in the attack against Paul and Silas, and the magistrates ordered them to be stripped and. beaten with rods. After they had been severely flogged, they were thrown into prison and the jailer was commanded to guard them carefully. When he received these orders, he put them in the inner cell and fastened their feet in the stocks. About midnight Paul and Silas were praying and singing hymns to God and the other prisoners were listening to them. — Acts 16:22-25 (NIV)

Wait a minute. These brothers were doing the will of God and yet they were severely beaten. Some people have the mistaken idea that life will be picture-perfect as long as you are doing the will of God. And yet we learn from the

Bible that that's clearly not the case. In fact, you might get into worse trouble as a result of doing God's will.

But here's the most amazing part of the story: These guys were bloody and broken, clearly in a lot of physical pain after being severely beaten, chained to the walls in a maximum security prison, and yet at midnight they sent beautiful hymns of praise wafting through the dungeon for all the prisoners to hear. Paul and Silas were communing with their Savior, praying and singing and offering praise to God.

Here's another lesson we can't let slip by: When we feel like we're all alone — beaten and abandoned at the bottom of a pit — we are not alone. Other prisoners are all around us. Neighbors and coworkers and strangers are all bound in their own darkness. Our Lord wants them to look at us, beaten down and broken, and say, "What's up with you? Shouldn't you be cursing God, same as everybody else? Why do you get to pray and sing while we are hurting and miserable?"

At this point we see what it means to glory in suffering. Only at this point can we truly show people what it means to praise and thank God in all circumstances. Only then can we show the world what true joy looks like.

That's why Peter wrote:

But you are a chosen generation, a royal priesthood, a holy nation, His own special people, that you may proclaim the praises of Him who called you out of darkness into His marvelous light;. — 1 Peter 2:9

You have been chosen "that you may proclaim the praises of Him who called you out of darkness into His marvelous light." God has put you on display so you can show the world His light. We are showing them what it looks like to nurture the fruit of joy. We are showing them the joy of abiding in Christ. We are showing them that circumstances cannot control us when we have joy.

The story of Paul and Silas shows that the world can't take away what it didn't give. Your joy comes from God so don't give it away. People can cause a lot of pain — especially those who loved you and turned their backs on you — but they can't take your joy, so maybe it's time to let those people go. Tell him you'll be better off without him. Stop clinging onto baggage you're better off without.

You may feel as if someone has kicked you to the curb and tossed you in a prison but that doesn't mean you're a prisoner. They can never touch the things that truly matter, like joy. You are free to choose joy. If your circumstances look like prison, start singing. Start praying and praising. Let the world know that God is still up to something good in your life.

Cultivate happiness, but when you can't have happiness, let the joy of the Lord be your strength.

Abide in the Lord and you will bear much fruit!

Peace

*But the fruit of the
Spirit is love, joy, **peace**,
longsuffering, kindness,
goodness, faithfulness,
gentleness and self-control.
— Galatians 5:22-23*

God wants to bless each one of His children with an abiding peace that surpasses all human understanding (Philippians 4:7). What is peace? ***Peace is inner calm and wellbeing, no matter the circumstances.***

No matter what is happening around you or in you, the Holy Spirit wants to cultivate the fruit of peace in your heart and mind. This is critical to your well-being in God's abundant life. You may be surrounded by trouble and turmoil. Enemies may be setting traps all around you but God wants to give you peace. The Holy Spirit wants to cultivate in you the ability to be spiritually, mentally and emotionally on top of things, even during the stormy times of life.

Have you noticed how difficulties pile up sometimes? They come in waves, mounting up, causing more and more turmoil. Sometimes it seems as if it's all going to cave in.

Thankfully, God has already equipped you with the means to be victorious. When the challenges of life come crashing down all around you, He enables you to not be buried, but to remain standing on top. Like a surfer, you can stay calm and cool as the waves roll underfoot. You can have that kind of peace no matter what comes your way. Troubles, trials and enemies need not smother you. God gives you the ability to stay calm and manage life no matter what's going on around you.

This is the peace that comes from God. It's not just any kind of peace. This is a spiritual peace that is beyond all explanation. It is a peace that doesn't even make sense in the natural. It's a peace that makes people stop and notice. When people see your inner peace against the backdrop of overwhelming challenges, they will know that God is doing something miraculous in your life. Some will even wonder why you're not losing your mind. They will see that God has given you a peace that defies human explanation.

The Practicality of Peace

God's peace that surpasses understanding has three important characteristics. The first characteristic is that it's practical.

Why is it practical?

Because this peace allows you to demonstrate your trust in God no matter what happens. Nothing can rob you of this peace because your life is hidden with Christ. Whatever comes against you has to go through God to get to you. As you abide in Christ, you receive nourishment from the vine. You continue bearing fruit, no matter what storms might come against you.

When your trust is in God, you can do better than wish or hope that you will make it through the storms. When your trust is in God, you will have the full assurance of peace because you are anchored by faith to God and His word. In Mark 4, Jesus spoke to the wind and waves and so can you. Tell your circumstances that they will not bury you and rob you of peace and joy. Christ is standing on top of your circumstances, so choose to remain on top with Him. Say, "It looks like the enemy is trying to take me out but I will not allow him to rob me of the things that matter most. I refuse to go under. I will abide in Christ. With God I will remain on top."

Every now and then you need to talk to the enemy. If that seems strange, remember that he's talking to you all the time. The Bible calls Satan the accuser of the brethren (Revelations 12:10). When he accuses you of all manner of wrongs and says you're going under, tell him, "You're talking to the wrong person. My Father has promised that I'll come out of this. I'm not enjoying this season of my life but I'm coming out of this. I don't like what I'm going through but with the Lord, I will be victorious in the end. Storms may rage but I'm coming out of this."

The practicality of peace is discovered by practicing two levels of trust.

First, we put our trust in God's word.

When we put our trust in God's word, He gives us an

inner peace and calm and a sense of wellbeing. We see Jesus modeling this peace for us in the following story from the Gospel of Mark:

On the same day, when evening had come, He said to them, "Let us cross over to the other side." Now when they had left the multitude, they took Him along in the boat as He was. And other little boats were also with Him. And a great windstorm arose and the waves beat into the boat so that it was already filling. But He was in the stern, asleep on a pillow. And they awoke Him and said to Him, "Teacher, do you not care that we are perishing?"

Then He arose and rebuked the wind and said to the sea, "Peace, be still!" And the wind ceased and there was a great calm. But He said to them, "Why are you so fearful? How is it that you have no faith?" And they feared exceedingly and said to one another, "Who can this be that even the wind and the sea obey Him!" — Mark 4:35-41

It's interesting to note that Jesus said, "Let's cross over," even though storms were common there and He knew they were headed into trouble. He didn't say, "Has anybody checked out the weather report? Did you watch Channel Two? Do you think it's safe? Do you all feel good about starting out?" He didn't even say, "Let's give it a try. We'll start out but if the weather picks up, I have a backup plan. We'll turn around and come back here." No! He said, "Let us cross over to the other side."

The Lord still works the same way today. He says, "I'd like you to go over there and do so-and-so. You need to cross that sea so you can accomplish my purpose."

Then when we hear those words, the excuses start to kick in. "It might not be safe. It won't be easy. Storms might come. We don't have a back-up plan." When the Lord gives directions, stop making excuses and start moving!

We see this principle in action in the life of Abram, who was later called Abraham, the father of the Jewish nation:

Now the Lord had said to Abram, "Get out of your country, from your family and from your father's house, to a land that I will show you." — Genesis 12:1

God didn't tell Abram where he was going. He didn't give him a complete picture. He just said, "Get up and go," and the Bible says that Abram got up and went.

This is the key to success. If God says it, just do it. He will answer questions along the way. He will bring peace. Don't try to get God to give you a full report before you start. If God says it, just do it.

That's what the disciples did at the Sea of Galilee. They set out in a larger boat with Jesus, but the Bible also says that "other little boats also went with him." Jesus had a lot more followers than the twelve disciples. He had several hundred others who followed Him around, experiencing healings and listening to His teachings. So a number of other followers of Jesus launched out after Him in watercraft that the Bible describes as "little boats."

The lesson here is not to worry about the size of your boat. You might think you don't have much to offer, but go ahead and follow Jesus anyway. Reject the temptation to compare yourself with other people's boats. And quit trying to buy a boat you can't afford! You may even see folk in a big boat laughing at you, saying, "Oh, is that your little boat? Ha, ha!"

Don't sweat those folk. People get to thinking that big houses and fancy cars are better; that big churches are more important; that you need a lot of resources to get God's work done. That's not how it works in God's kingdom. Thankfully, He accomplishes His work with much or little. All He needs is a willing heart. Little is much in God's kingdom. God can do big works with little vessels. Your little boat sails on the same sea as the big ones. You are all about the Father's business, no matter what the exteriors look like.

Mark 4:37 says, "And a great windstorm arose and the waves beat into the boat so that it was already filling." Do you think this storm caught Jesus off guard? Absolutely not! He knew. That's why He wanted to cross over in the first place. He knew a storm was coming.

God works in the same way today. He sends us into storms. But why? Because He is always teaching. He wants us to learn things we could never learn if we didn't encounter storms. He wants to give us a peace that surpasses understanding. Everything in life has something to do with a lesson. We can learn from all of life's circumstances.

Some people say, "Everything happens for a reason," but that's not biblical. All bad things are not "meant to be" in God's good plan. Here's what the Bible says:

And we know that all things work together for good to those who love God, to those who are the called according to His purpose. — Romans 8:28

The Bible does not say that "everything was supposed to happen." It doesn't even say that all things work together for good *for everyone*. It says that God will make things work out for good in the end "for those who love God."

When a horrible tragedy happens, it didn't "happen for a reason," as if God is in the business of trying to ruin people's lives. It happened because the devil wanted it to happen! When bad things happen because of people's wrongful choices, they weren't "meant to happen." They happened because the sinful flesh wanted them to happen.

Bad things often happen simply because we live in a crazy world. Some things happen without an explanation at all. We can't know why everything happens, so we need to get on with living the life of faith. We need to trust God because He will take everything that happens and make it a lesson. Bad things shouldn't have happened but He can find a way to make them work out for good in the end for His people.

In Mark 4:29, we see how Jesus was asleep on a pillow in the rear of the boat. Wait. Seriously?! This storm was so overwhelming that the boat was starting to sink. And if it was that bad in the big boat, you can imagine how horrifying it would be for the folk in the little boats. You can imagine how people would have been blaming Jesus, desperately hoping He would do something about it. After all, He's the one who told them to cross over! And this is just like Jesus, to be sound asleep on a pillow at the back of the boat with not a care in the world.

From a human perspective, this doesn't make any sense. But in the spiritual realm, Jesus is showing us what peace looks like. At a time when you ought to be losing your mind, He can instead give you sleep. He'll say, "It's alright. Trust me. You can go to sleep now."

Have you ever been at sea in a boat during a storm? It happened to me once when a preacher friend offered to take us out fishing. His boat was on a beautiful part of the sea so we said, "Sure. That sounds fun. Let's go out." I was only a little concerned when he suggested we leave after dark, but he convinced us that the fishing would be better then.

As the night progressed, we had a wonderful time hanging out and talking and making new friends. But then all of sudden, the wind and the waves started to pick up. I got a little concerned but my friend didn't seem to mind.

"I've been out in a lot worse weather than this," he assured me. "If you start to feel seasick, just take in the fresh air. Breathe deep. You'll learn to handle it."

Meanwhile, some of the brothers were actually throwing out their lines and trying to catch fish during all this chaos. As for me, I was doing all I could to stay focused and not lose it. Mostly I was thinking how badly I wanted to stand on solid ground.

The squall kept on for some time before subsiding, and as it turned out, only one person got sick. And it was my friend, the owner. And boy, did he get sick! It wasn't a little upset stomach. No! I can still see my man leaning over the side of the boat, feeding the fish over and over again. Eventually he got himself back together and we were happy to catch a few fish. We even caught a small shark that his wife cooked the next day.

If that's ever happened to you, you know how horrifying it feels. The deck keeps shifting under your feet. Your insides keep going up and down. All you long for is something solid under your feet. Any place on terra firma is better than that.

Now imagine Jesus stretched out on a pillow and sleeping like a baby through all of that. It's crazy!

"We are about to die," the disciples said, "and don't you even care?"

They didn't understand that Jesus never stops caring. They didn't understand that He is never *not* in control. Even when the waves and wind are raging, He is in charge of the storm.

Be encouraged. You may not know it but God is in control of everything. He may not have started the storm but He is in charge if you let Him. It doesn't matter whose "fault" it is. He can still take charge of everything you go through. He can speak to what's messing with you.

Then He arose and rebuked the wind.

"Rebuke" is a strong word. It's not a suggestion. It's a *command* that comes from authority. Only those who have the ability to control things can rebuke them. Jesus was in control of the wind so He rebuked it. He was in control of the sea so He said, "Peace, be still."

And the wind ceased and there was a great calm.

This describes a peace too miraculous to understand. God may not choose to physically stop the storm in your life but He is more than able to bring a great calm so you can experience peace during and after the storm.

Let's pause here to look at the questions Jesus asked and to see how they apply to us today. Jesus asked, "Why are you so fearful? How is it that you have no faith? You all have been with me for a long time. You heard me teach and you saw the miracles. Then we get out here and all of a sudden you panic. Isn't this what I've been telling you about? Why are you so surprised when miracles occur? Why are you so afraid? Don't you understand that I'm in charge? Why are you so worried?"

Jesus is asking the same questions today. He came into your life. He's on your ship, no matter what happens. You might think He's checked out. You might say, "Why are you sleeping? Don't you see that I'm going under? You know that I've been praying about this forever and I still haven't gotten an answer."

Even if God seems to be asleep, He's not. In the words of the old hymn:

Master, the tempest is raging.
The billows are tossing high.
The sky is o'ershadowed with blackness,
No shelter or help is nigh;
Carest thou not that we perish?
How canst thou lie asleep,
When each moment so madly is threat'ning
A grave in the angry deep?

The winds and the waves shall obey thy will.
"Peace, be still."
Whether the wrath of the storm-tossed sea,
Or struggles or evil, whatever it be,
No water can swallow the ship where lies
the Master of ocean and earth and skies:
They all shall sweetly obey thy will.
"Peace, be still! Peace, be still."
They all shall sweetly obey thy will.
"Peace, peace, be still."[9]

If you are going through a storm, know that Jesus is on board and He is not panicked. You might feel alone but you're not. When you got saved, He didn't come into your life just to keep you from going to hell, so don't treat salvation as fire insurance. He cares as much about your life on earth as He does about your life after death. He doesn't want to leave you alone for this part of the journey. Salvation is as much about the present as it is the future. You need help getting through this crazy world and He is

---

[9] Mary Ann Baker, "Master, the Tempest is Raging," 1874, Public Domain.

ready to give it.

Jesus says, "When I came to take up residence in you, I came to take charge. That means you don't have to worry when the storms come. They don't catch me by surprise. Put your trust in me. Be at peace. I will get you through the storms."

At times the waves will threaten to capsize your boat but be at peace. At times your life will be confusing but be at peace. Don't be like the super-spiritual Christian who says, "Well, I was fellowshipping with the Lord this morning and He explained to me why I was going through this troubling time. Then as we communed at lunch, He was enlightening me to the mysteries of ..."

It's okay to be clueless about your circumstances! Besides, He has a lot of things He could say, but mostly He is silent. He's not in the habit of sitting and talking folk through their days. More often, He teaches through long seasons of silence. That's how we discover His promises. That's how we learn to trust His word.

When you find yourself in the midst of a storm, you don't need a phone call or email from God. You already have His word. He has promised to be with you and to carry you through to the other side. He gives you peace and joy. You don't need to look for a new word from God so much as you need to remember the words He already gave you.

When God called me and my family to California in 1989, He said I'd be preaching to thousands. And yet our little church began with 34 people. After a year, we had grown to 45. When they held a first year anniversary banquet for me, they had the nerve to be happy. Those folk were so excited at what God was doing with 45 people.

I still remember driving to that banquet in Sunnyvale with an attitude. I was grouching to my wife, saying "Why are we here? What is there to celebrate? We brought in 11 new people in 12 months. Wow. Now I have to sit and look at these grinning people and eat dried chicken."

Thankfully, Meredith had more faith than me. She calmed me down, reminding me to trust God's word. The problem is, we focus on the challenges when they arise. We look at the deficiencies when we don't see manifestations of God's promises. Why do we look at the deficiencies when we should be looking to God's promises and His provision?

First learn to trust His word. That's the first level of trust that leads to peace. But it's not all.

Second, learn to trust His silence.

Trusting in His silence means experiencing joy and peace when He is not saying anything, even in the midst of great uncertainty. One very helpful approach is to take up prayer and fasting. "Turn your plate down," the saints used to say. Pray and fast, but don't put any expectations on God, because sometimes He will sit and silently watch you pray, fast, speak in another tongue and more. God is God and He may choose to remain silent, despite your most ardent display of begging and pleading.

Why won't God say anything?!

Because He's teaching you. If you could hear His thoughts, you'd hear Him say, "Even when I'm not talking, I'm still here. Even when I'm not revealing, I'm still here. Even when I'm not reacting like you think I should, I'm still here. I will never leave you. My love, peace and joy are available to you, so abide in me."

Peace is practical for times like that. God's peace will carry you through your worst seasons. That's the practicality of peace.

The Prerequisites of Peace

If you want God's peace, know that it has some prerequisites. You can't just "get it" with no strings attached. You have to do some things to get peace. It has some conditions.

Hopefully you have already learned that you can't claim God's promises without meeting the conditions. We talked about that in the context of John 15:16 and how you can't treat God like a vending machine. Don't expect to receive anything you want from God unless you first abide in Him and conform your desires to His desires.

Christians in today's world are always claiming something. We are the *name it, claim it* generation of Christians and we have the nerve to try and claim any old thing. I've seen broke folk who can't even pay their bills go to the dealership and say, "I claim that Benz in the name of Jesus." Why not claim the ability to discipline your life? God never promised us fancy wheels and bling. Don't be like the woman who came home with a car full of stuff and a huge debt, saying "I had to get it all. The sign said, 'Everything must go!'" Don't do it! Let it go to other people's houses.

When God gives a promise, look at the conditions first. The same thing is true when it comes to peace. God promised peace, but there are some prerequisites.

What are the prerequisites of peace?

We find the answer to that question in Paul's letter to the Philippians:

Rejoice in the Lord always. Again I will say, rejoice! Let your gentleness be known to all men. The Lord is at hand. Be anxious for nothing, but in everything by prayer and supplication, with thanksgiving, let your requests be made known to God; and the peace of God, which surpasses all understanding, will guard your hearts and minds through Christ Jesus. — Philippians 4:4-7

For the God of peace to be with you — to possess "the peace of God, which surpasses all understanding" — Paul gives us several conditions that are prerequisites to peace.

First Paul says "Rejoice." And in case we missed it the first time, "Again I will say, rejoice!" If you want to qualify for peace, learn to be joyful. Cultivate a lifestyle of joy. We already talked about joy, the second fruit of the Spirit. Joy doesn't depend on what happens. Joy is not reactionary. Joy is proactive. Joy is a choice. Joy comes when you set your affections on God and rejoice in the God of your salvation. You may find it impossible to rejoice in the black clouds and crashing waves, but you can still rejoice in the Lord who holds you in the palm of His hand.

Rejoice always. Be like King David who wrote in the Psalms:

I will bless the Lord at all times; His praise shall continually be in my mouth. — Psalm 34:1

To obtain peace, cultivate a lifestyle of joy.

The second condition of peace found in Philippians 4 is a lifestyle of gentleness toward others. "Let your gentleness be known to all men. The Lord is at hand." We will learn more about this fruit of the Spirit in the Gentleness chapter. First, let's talk about what gentleness is *not*.

You may know someone — not you, of course! — who is always pressuring folk to act right or do better or perform. They are not at peace because they want other people around them to change. It's uncomfortable for everyone, because their closest family and friends are all paying for the fact that this person is on a mission. It's as if they don't want to be miserable all alone so they drag others into it to share the misery.

Don't be hard on others just because your life isn't easy. Don't feel entitled to an attitude because *you* are going through tough times.

To cash in on God's promise of peace, let your gentleness be known to everyone. Let folks know that although *life* is difficult, *you* aren't. Say, "I refuse to be difficult to others. I'm going to be gentle. I'm going to be meek. I'm going to be humble. I'm going to stop making people miserable. I'm going to show people how to thank God for good in difficult circumstances and to cultivate a lifestyle of joy."

To experience peace, we need, first, to cultivate a lifestyle of joy.

Second, we need a lifestyle of gentleness toward others.

Third, we need a lifestyle of prayer.

Be anxious for nothing, but in everything by prayer and supplication, with thanksgiving, let your requests be made known to God.

I love that verse. The New Living Translation reads, "Don't worry about anything. Instead, pray about everything." It's so simple.

Don't worry.

Instead, pray about everything you are tempted to worry about.

Worry is futile. It does nothing good. Think about all the hours you spent worrying and what came of it. *Nothing!* It only made things worse, as the worry got to your nerves, muscles, face and bad feelings. Worry gets in your face and takes away the beauty that should be there. You shouldn't try to bear the burdens that only God can bear. Worry is a heavy burden that will break your back.

Remember what Jesus said in the Sermon on the

Mount:

> *"Therefore I say to you, do not worry about your life,*
> *what you will eat or what you will drink; nor about*
> *your body, what you will put on. Is not life more than*
> *food and the body more than clothing? Look at the*
> *birds of the air, for they neither sow nor reap nor*
> *gather into barns; yet your heavenly Father feeds them.*
> *Are you not of more value than they? Which of you by*
> *worrying can add one cubit to his stature?*

> *"So why do you worry about clothing? Consider the*
> *lilies of the field, how they grow: they neither toil nor*
> *spin; and yet I say to you that even Solomon in all his*
> *glory was not arrayed like one of these. Now if God so*
> *clothes the grass of the field, which today is, and*
> *tomorrow is thrown into the oven, will He not much*
> *more clothe you, O you of little faith?*

> *"Therefore do not worry, saying, 'What shall we eat?'*
> *or 'What shall we drink?' or 'What shall we wear?'*
> *For after all these things the Gentiles seek. For your*
> *heavenly Father knows that you need all these things.*
> *But seek first the kingdom of God and His*
> *righteousness, and all these things shall be added to*
> *you. Therefore do not worry about tomorrow, for*
> *tomorrow will worry about its own things. Sufficient for*
> *the day is its own trouble."* — Matthew 6:25-34

Don't worry! Worry is futile! It does nothing good.
Instead of worry, pray. Pray about everything you would
worry about. Cultivate a lifestyle of prayer. Pray at all
times, no matter what you are doing. And when you pray,
pray with thanksgiving.

Always be joyful.
Always be gentle.
Always pray.

Pray in the context of joyfulness. Have an attitude of gratitude, no matter what challenges may come up against you. Give every moment over to the Lord. Don't heap stuff on your shoulders. Shovel it onto God.

Have an attitude of gratitude when you go to bed at night, when you get up in the morning and when you're driving in the car. Pray about everything. Say, "Lord, these people are testing my nerves. I'm giving them to you right now, Jesus. Give me patience. Give me gentleness. I'm going into a situation that could get testy. Take these challenges off my shoulders. I need your help, Lord. Things will go south if I let my emotions take charge. If you don't help me here, Lord, I may have to call Pastor and say, 'Come get me out, Pastor. I'm in county.'"

Give it all to the Lord before it gets bad. Pray, pray, pray all the time. With joy and gentleness, constantly give your challenges over to the Lord.

The fourth prerequisite to peace is found in Philippians 4, as well as this verse from the book of Isaiah:

You will keep in perfect peace those whose minds are steadfast, because they trust in you.— Isaiah 26:3 (NIV)

To find peace, keep your mind on God. Keep your mind on good things. No matter what circumstances you are going through, keep your mind stayed on God. This is reinforced in the section of scripture following what we just read from Philippians 4:

Finally, brethren, whatever things are true, whatever things are noble, whatever things are just, whatever things are pure, whatever things are lovely, whatever things are of good report, if there is any virtue and if there is anything praiseworthy — meditate on these things. The things which you learned and received and heard and saw in me, these do and the God of peace will be with you. — Philippians 4:8-9

Paul tells us to meditate on whatever is true, noble, just, pure, lovely, of good report, virtuous and praiseworthy. This is a condition of peace. If you want to experience this mind-blowing peace — this peace that defies explanation — then fix your mind on the right stuff. You cannot grow this kind of peace if your mind is planted in garbage. If your head is filled with nonsense, you won't know this peace.

Stop for a moment and consider how the entertainment industry often fills your mind with the wrong stuff. There was a time when television shows taught the difference between good and bad — how truth and justice prevailed — with heroes like the Lone Ranger, Tonto and a horse named Silver. No matter what predicament they got into, they always came out on the good side. We saw how trouble didn't last.

I still remember being a kid, watching TV on Saturday morning with our high-water pajamas on. Every hero taught us that good prevailed and trouble didn't last. Batman would get pushed to the brink of destruction and then he'd pull a special gizmo from his bat-belt to get himself and Robin through. That belt had every kind of technology that the 1960s could imagine! We were learning that if we did the right thing, we would make it in the end.

Contrast that with reality shows where one bumbling group of idiots is replaced by another that's even worse than the first. The vast majority of entertainment is useless. It's worse than a waste of time. People of destiny have more productive things to do with their lives. We have meaningful lives to live. We have useful things to do. Why would we present ourselves like pupils to teachers who show us how to be dumb? The best thing I've learned is to record programs in advance so I can fast-forward through the dumb parts. I'm tired of letting trash into my mind.

Garbage in ... garbage out.

To know God's perfect peace, cultivate a lifestyle of joy, gentleness, prayer and a mind fixed on God. These are the prerequisites of peace.

The Promises Regarding Peace

We have studied the practicality of peace. We have looked at the prerequisites of peace. That brings us to the promises of peace.

Philippians 4:7 says, "and the peace of God, which surpasses all understanding, will guard your hearts and minds through Christ Jesus."

Don't miss the nuances of this text. God is saying that if you meet the conditions, He will send a security guard — a military force, if necessary — to assure that you will experience His perfect peace. You don't have to worry when opposition comes or when the devil tries to assail you. Peace will already be at the ready, guarding what's most important in your life.

Why? Because Philippians 4 says that God's peace will guard your heart and mind.

When trouble comes, Peace says, "Hold up a minute. Do you have a pass? You can't go making trouble here. You're too disruptive. You don't have the right agenda. This is a place of love, joy and peace. We have patience and long-suffering here. This is where the joy of the Lord is our strength. You can't come up in here."

... and the peace of God will guard your hearts and minds ...

Meet the conditions of peace and that peace will get you through the worst that the enemy has to offer. God's peace gives you the ability to sail on troubled seas. Other folk will think you ought to be drowning by now, but you're still in charge and all together, saying "I'm still standing because God gave me the peace that surpasses human understanding."

That's the kind of testimony that will bring God glory. It's a testimony that the world needs to see. It's a testimony of folk like you and me who should have been wrecked on the rocks. By the grace of God, were still sailing. We need to testify about the glorious God who can work these kinds of miracles in the world today.

Can you have that kind of testimony?

Yes you can! By faith, you can stand on the solid promises of God. Let the world hear you say, "The enemy has beaten me down and messed me over, but the Lord has rescued me every time. My enemies have tried to knock me down, but God has lifted me up. God alone is responsible for the joy and peace you see on my face. And if He did that for me, He can do the same for you."

God alone is responsible for the joy and peace we experience. Let God bless you and let His peace guard your heart and mind, so you don't end up looking like what you've been through. He can make you look so good that they'll never believe the kind of hell you've experienced. My prayer is that you will possess an abundance of love, joy and peace, as you draw near to God and cultivate the beautiful fruit of His Spirit in your life.

Abide in the Lord and you will bear much fruit!

Longsuffering

*But the fruit of the Spirit is love, joy, peace, **longsuffering**, kindness, goodness, faithfulness, gentleness and self-control.*
— Galatians 5:22-23

The Greek word that Paul uses in Galatians 5 for *longsuffering* is *makrothumia*. While some Bible translators have rendered the word as "patience," the meaning has more nuances than that. "Longsuffering" is a more accurate rendering.

This is our two-part definition for longsuffering: ***Longsuffering is, first, patience and contentment despite irritations, inconveniences and inactivity; and second, the ability to put up with other people even when they're doing wrong, being difficult or causing provocation.***

To better understand this fruit of the Spirit, consider the antithesis of longsuffering ... which is *provocation*. Folk with this negative anointing know how to work your nerves like nobody's business. They study you and say, "Well, look at that. There's some nerves I haven't worked in a while. Let me go ahead and fool with those ones."

People with this special anointing wait until life has frayed you down to your last nerve. You're one step from utter breakdown but you still have that one last nerve. It's tucked away, not normally in operation, but you've kept it there in reserve. So when life has beat you up and you're hanging on by a thread, these special folk come along and tap dance on that thread. They trample your last nerve.

At times like that, it's not enough to have an average amount of patience. You need God's mighty fruit of longsuffering. This, in turn, will give you access to the full package of love, joy, peace and all the other fruit of the Spirit.

One of the most fundamental gardening truths is that fruit needs to be well-cultivated. When you transplant a fruit tree, you have the potential for fruit. But potential is not enough. You still have to cultivate it. You need to invest in it, which means giving it cultivation and nutrients. You need to give it time to develop and mature. It needs the right temperature and the right amount of moisture. Only diligent cultivation will enable it to develop a fruit that's worth eating.

The same principle applies to the fruit of the Spirit. Just because you are saved doesn't mean you will automatically bear fruit. Godly character can only develop when you are cultivated by the Holy Spirit. If the Lord doesn't do a work on the inside when irritations and inconveniences arise, you will still manifest ungodliness on the outside. Just because you've been saved twenty-some years doesn't mean God's fruit is mature in you. You may be acting in your anointing one minute, then respond out of the Spirit the next. The fruit will not be active if you haven't cultivated it.

Don't mistake your anointing for maturity. Be grateful that God has gifted you, but remember that receiving God's anointing doesn't make you mature. You need cultivation. You need to give the Holy Spirit full control over every area of your life.

I knew a pastor once who was driving home from an anointed service when somebody cut him off and almost caused a significant accident. The pastor had to swerve to keep from getting crushed. So he sped up and followed that car, driving several miles out of his way until it stopped at a red light. That's when the pastor jumped out and unloaded all his verbal rage on that driver, telling him how he nearly killed some folk and he ought to get out of the car now so he could teach him a thing or two.

Then the Holy Spirit spoke to my friend and said, "If he gets out, what are you going to do? What's your plan? Get into a bloody battle? Call your church members so they can bail you out of jail?"

This pastor may have been anointed but he hadn't been cultivated with the power of the Holy Spirit. He needed the fruit of love, joy, peace and especially longsuffering.

Be Proactive within your Circle of Influence

Irritations and inconveniences are inevitable. People and situations will annoy you. You cannot get through life without a generous amount of irritations and inconveniences. But while you can't avoid them, you *can* prepare for them. You can be proactive.

In fact, some irritations and inconveniences can be corrected and eliminated if you are proactive. You can take some steps in advance to make things better when trials and tribulations arise.

"Be Proactive" is the first principle covered by Stephen Covey in his best-selling book, *The 7 Habits of Highly Effective People*.[10] This is not a Christian book, but when I first studied it, I saw how the concepts were biblical. I was able to apply all seven habits to scriptural principles.

So the first habit of highly effective people is to be proactive. That means you don't wait for life to happen to you. You don't sit back and expect God to do all your work for you. You take responsibility for each moment and shape your circumstances to take you to better places. Yes, many things are out of your control. Yes, there are some things that only God can do but there are also many things that He expects you to do.

Take a moment right now to consider your concerns. You have a list of things that you're tempted to worry about. You have situations that you hope will improve. You have unresolved issues. You have unfulfilled needs. If you're honest, you can probably come up with a full list of things that are not as you want them to be. These are your concerns.

In your mind — or on piece of paper — draw a circle

___

[10] Stephen Covey, *The 7 Habits of Highly Effective People* (New York: Simon & Schuster [Free Press], 1989).

around all these concerns. This is what Stephen Covey calls your "Circle of concern."

Now draw a smaller circle around all of the concerns that you are able to influence or change. This is called your "Circle of influence." Outside of this circle of influence will be the concerns that you are powerless to change or influence. It's those things that you should ask God to influence because you are powerless in those areas.

For example, natural disasters like hurricanes and earthquakes are outside of your circle of influence. You may be concerned about them but you can't do anything to stop them. But here's the good news: Your *attitude* toward natural disasters is within your circle of influence.

So first, learn how to divide your concerns into those things that are within your circle of influence and those that aren't. Second, learn how to pray for the things you can't change. When something is outside of your circle of influence, ask God to work because there's nothing you can do about it. Pray too for things within your circle of influence, but don't expect Him to take charge of those things. You already know that God wants you to take responsibility for those things, so your prayers are more for wisdom and guidance and strength and perseverance.

Here's an example: If you were going on your dream vacation, you'd likely be concerned about the weather. This is a concern that is outside of your circle of influence. You can't change the weather by worrying about it, so you pray, "Lord, bless us with a wonderful vacation. We pray that the weather is great, but if it's not, help us to have a wonderful time anyway."

Here's a second example: Suppose you're hoping to find a godly spouse and get married in the next year. Is this within your circle of influence? Absolutely not. You'll find yourself in a world of trouble if you push and shove to make that happen. Yes, you can take careful steps toward meeting kingdom-first individuals and being involved with godly singles. Get plugged into an online dating service if you like. But mostly pray, because the results are out of your control. Take care to live by God's word, not playing games with scripture out of desperation. Ask God to give you the desires of your heart but don't treat Him like a genie in a bottle. Your prayer list might include 6' 2", 205 pounds of muscle and a six figure income, but all of that's out of your control. Don't live in a dream bubble, as if you're an actor in that classic television show Fantasy Island. Instead say, "Lord, I'd love to get married. I believe I'd make a great marriage partner with the right individual. God, I'm open to you causing my path to cross with the right person who is first and foremost committed to you."

Here's a third example: Maybe you have no personal support system. A personal support system is a network of activities and relationships that nurture and sustain you. They fill you up, as opposed to people and activities that drain you. Everyone has drainers in the workplace and at home. Even kids can be drainers, with all the energy they require from you. Godly parenting is impossible without the fruit of longsuffering, because these kids are anointed some days to try your patience. So everybody needs fillers to help deal with the drainers.

A personal support system is a need that God has given you control of, so this is within your circle of influence. It is up to you to do something about it. Do more than pray. Go find the activities that recharge you. Take up hobbies or recreational activities that you enjoy. Build up an inner circle of friends who can support you as you support them. Make an investment of time and energy, getting to know these friends on a deeper level. You can't have deeply-committed relationships without doing the work of laying the foundation. Ask God for help finding the people you can pull into your crew. Be like Jesus, who had a crew of close friends that included Mary, Martha, Lazarus, Peter, James and John. He didn't have everybody on His crew and neither can you. These are people who see the real you, even when you are at your worst. They are folk you can call any time of day or night and they will drop everything to help you. If someone says they can't be that kind of friend, believe them and keep looking. Upgrade your personal support system because this is within your circle of influence.

As a fourth example, suppose you have a personal support system but those people aren't meeting your felt needs anymore. This often happens when the covenant you made with each other in the past has faded away or gotten neglected. This happens all the time with marriage relationships, when the passions cool and the years go by. This is still in your circle of influence, which means it's time to renew that covenant. It's time to review the commitment you made to each other.

We see this regularly with married couples who

publically renew their wedding vows. It's a time to declare that you and your spouse have changed … that you're not the same people who walked down the aisle … that your skills and priorities and experiences have been growing and shifting, which means you are different than you were when you got married. There's nothing wrong with that, so don't blame your spouse for changing. Your spouse is growing into this new season of life and so are you. Don't get on her case because she doesn't call you all the time and give you the same attention she did before she had a baby sitting on her lap. Life shifts sometimes so roll with it. That doesn't mean you can't love each other the same.

Whether it's your spouse or your close friends, the time will come to sit down and revisit that covenant you made with each other. Ask some questions to see if you are providing for their felt needs and let them know how they can do the same for you. Asking questions is the opposite of barking out demands. You don't motivate your personal support system by barking. You may want to come home and kick your shoes off in front of the sport's center, but that's not serving your spouse.

Here's a fifth example of something that's within your circle of influence: Maybe you're tired of being overweight. You might think this is out of your control, when in fact you can move it into your circle of influence. Make the decision to change this. I know, because I spent most of my adult life overweight. In so many ways, aging works against your best intentions. With the advice of my doctor, I have become more intentional about diet and exercise. If you have walked this road, you know how miserable it is to carry all that extra weight around. Personally, I reached the bottom when I had to go buy a new suit because none of my old ones fit anymore. I was sick of myself so I said, "Something has got to change." Thankfully I'm on a journey to a better place now.

Be intentional and improve your weight and your health within your circle of influence. You have to do it with intention. Don't ask yourself how you *feel* about it, because your feelings have nothing to do with it. Don't ask your feelings what you want to eat or drink. Your doctor will tell you to drink no less than a half-gallon of water each day. Your doctor will tell you to lay off the junk foods, eat more fruits and vegetables and get some good exercise. You have to tell your body what to do so your feelings won't get in the way.

In summary, learn to rightly divide the world of truth. Be intentional about dealing with the concerns that are within your circle of influence, while not stressing over those concerns that are outside your influence.

Patience and Contentment Despite Irritations and Inconveniences

The fruit of longsuffering is especially designed for those times when people are provoking us or working evil against us. That's what we learn from the Greek word for longsuffering, which is *makrothumia*. This describes an attitude of patience and contentment despite irritations and inconveniences, especially when people are intent upon provoking us.

For a deeper understanding, look at the story of Hannah, who was unable to have a child with her husband Elkanah:

Now there was a certain man of Ramathaim Zophim, of the mountains of Ephraim and his name was Elkanah the son of Jeroham, the son of Elihu, the son of Tohu, the son of Zuph, an Ephraimite. And he had two wives: the name of one was Hannah and the name of the other Peninnah. Peninnah had children, but Hannah had no children.

This man went up from his city yearly to worship and sacrifice to the Lord of hosts in Shiloh. Also the two sons of Eli, Hophni and Phinehas, the priests of the Lord, were there. And whenever the time came for Elkanah to make an offering, he would give portions to Peninnah his wife and to all her sons and daughters. But to Hannah he would give a double portion, for he loved Hannah, although the Lord had closed her womb. And her rival also provoked her severely, to make her miserable, because the Lord had closed her womb.

So it was, year by year, when she went up to the house of the LORD, that she provoked her; therefore she wept and did not eat. Then Elkanah her husband said to her, "Hannah, why do you weep? Why do you not eat? And why is your heart grieved? Am I not better to you than ten sons?" — 1 Samuel 1:1-8

The Bible tells us that Hannah was loved by her husband Elkanah but she was barren. On the other hand, sister girl Peninah could kick out babies but she didn't have the same level of love from Elkanah. So Peninah thought,

"Hannah has the love that I want, but I have the babies she wants. So I know what I'm going do to get at her." Peninah came up with a plan to provoke Hannah and make her life miserable.

The same dynamics are at work in people's lives today. You have something good that someone else is in short supply of, so they provoke you. In their messed-up way of thinking, they remind you of your inadequacies. They set out to make your life miserable, even though it doesn't seem to make any sense. You still see women today doing what Peninah did, flaunting babies to provoke other desperate women with broken hearts. It's not fair but it happens.

The only hope for women and men of God is to embrace the fruit of longsuffering, while waiting for God to work His purpose out for good in the end. Sometimes the people and situations that irritate us are part of God's larger plan. We see that quite clearly in 1 Samuel, where God used Peninah's provocation for His own divine plan. Hannah actually had to be provoked "bad enough" to get the result that God wanted. While she was at the temple in Shiloh, Hannah cried so hard before the Lord that the priest thought she was drunk.

And she was in bitterness of soul and prayed to the Lord and wept in anguish. Then she made a vow and said, "O Lord of hosts, if you will indeed look on the affliction of your maidservant and remember me and not forget your maidservant, but will give your maidservant a male child, then I will give him to the

*Lord all the days of his life and no razor shall come
upon his head."
And it happened, as she continued praying before the
Lord, that Eli watched her mouth. Now Hannah spoke
in her heart; only her lips moved, but her voice was not
heard. Therefore Eli thought she was drunk. So Eli said
to her, "How long will you be drunk? Put your wine
away from you!"*

*But Hannah answered and said, "No, my lord, I am a
woman of sorrowful spirit. I have drunk neither wine
nor intoxicating drink, but have poured out my soul
before the Lord. Do not consider your maidservant a
wicked woman, for out of the abundance of my
complaint and grief I have spoken until now." Then Eli
answered and said, "Go in peace and the God of Israel
grant your petition which you have asked of Him." And
she said, "Let your maidservant find favor in your
sight." So the woman went her way and ate and her
face was no longer sad.*

*Then they rose early in the morning and worshiped
before the Lord and returned and came to their house
at Ramah. And Elkanah knew Hannah his wife and the
Lord remembered her. So it came to pass in the process
of time that Hannah conceived and bore a son and
called his name Samuel, saying, "Because I have asked
for him from the Lord."* — 1 Samuel 1:10-20

Hannah needed to be provoked enough to cry out to the
Lord like she did. God used her being provoked for a divine
purpose. He answered her prayer by giving her the baby
she wanted. He even blessed her with several other sons
and daughters after that. But even more important to God's
plan, her son Samuel became the prophet that led Israel

back to the Lord.

> *Now when she had weaned him, she took him up with
> her, with three bulls, one ephah of flour and a skin of
> wine and brought him to the house of the Lord in
> Shiloh. And the child was young. Then they slaughtered
> a bull and brought the child to Eli. And she said, "O my
> lord! As your soul lives, my lord, I am the woman who
> stood by you here, praying to the Lord. For this child I
> prayed and the Lord has granted me my petition which
> I asked of Him. Therefore I also have lent him to the
> Lord; as long as he lives he shall be lent to the Lord."
> So they worshiped the Lord there.* — 1 Samuel 1:24-28

Here we see Hannah fulfilling her promise to God, to
give her child back to the Lord. And that's what God
wanted all along. He didn't want to bless Hannah with a
baby so she could shove him in Peninah's face saying,
"Nah, nah nah! You're no better than me!"

God wants exactly the same commitment from you
today. When He causes something beautiful to be born in
your life, He needs you to give the child back to Him.
Samuel could only be unique because he was raised in the
temple. He proved that God's greatest plans can be rooted
in ugly provocation.

The fruit of the Spirit is longsuffering.

Conflict is an unavoidable part of your spiritual
training, so welcome it as God's tool for cultivating the
fruit of longsuffering in your life. When you feel God
working those muscles of patience and longsuffering, know
that it's an important part of your spiritual workout. You

can't strengthen a muscle by ignoring it. You get strong by working reps with that muscle, which will make you uncomfortable at times. But press on because of the coming glory. You and God will do some wonderful things with that patience and longsuffering. God is growing you, so thank God even for times of provocation. You might even want to send your enemy a message, saying, "I was thinking about you today. I just want to thank you for the positive role you play in my life. You are in my prayers."

That attitude takes the kind of courage that can only come from abiding close to the vine, Jesus Christ. Rejoice in His amazing gift of longsuffering.

Abide in the Lord and you will bear much fruit!

Kindness

*But the fruit of the
Spirit is love, joy, peace,
longsuffering, **kindness**,
goodness, faithfulness,
gentleness and self-control.*
— *Galatians 5:22-23*

The fifth fruit of the Spirit is one of the simplest to understand. It is simply kindness. It is benevolent action. God doesn't want us to just talk about kindness; *He wants us to be kind ... on purpose.*

Here's our definition for kindness: ***benevolence in action***.

Kindness is being good. It is being helpful. It is being generous. It is giving. It is not just words. You don't *tell* people you are kind. You *show* them you are kind.

Don't be too eager to tell people how nice you are or your actions may belie your words. You may "mean well," but it won't feel that way to others if you're not doing a good job of showing your benevolence in action. Don't let the evidence of your kindness be a well-guarded secret.

If somebody got arrested for being kind, they wouldn't need to say a word in their defense. Their motives would be clear by their benevolent actions. The evidence of true kindness would be obvious to everyone.

You've heard about "random acts of kindness" and there's absolutely nothing wrong with that. It's great to pay for a random stranger's tank of gas or basket of groceries. That's wonderful, but I believe the Holy Spirit wants to cultivate in us more than kindness toward strangers. He wants us to practice deliberate, intentional acts of kindness toward the people we know, as well as toward the people we don't know. Don't spend so much effort giving kindness to strangers that you neglect those who are closest to you. Practice deliberate, intentional acts of kindness toward friends, family, coworkers and strangers alike.

God is Kind

Let us look now at the biblical underpinnings of kindness. It all begins with the fact that God is kind. That's the foundation. God is kind and therefore we are kind. The Apostle Paul wrote:

> *And God raised us up with Christ and seated us with Him in the heavenly realms in Christ Jesus, in order that in the coming ages He might show the incomparable riches of His grace, expressed in His kindness to us in Christ Jesus. For it is by grace you have been saved, through faith — and this is not from yourselves, it is the gift of God — not by works, so that no one can boast.* — Ephesians 2:6-9 (NIV)

This is how God expressed His kindness towards us, in

the gift of His only begotten Son. He didn't just *say* He loved us. He *showed us* the exceeding riches of His grace, expressed in His kindness to us in Christ. In kindness, He saved us by grace through faith, not works. Nobody deserves salvation. Nobody is good enough. This is God's gift of kindness to all who wish to receive it.

When God sent His son to earth, He looked at us and smiled to think of how blessed we would be, despite the tremendous suffering Jesus would endure. In response — as we look at what Jesus did on Calvary — we ought to rejoice at God's amazing kindness, that while we were yet sinners and before we had even been born, God was expressing His ultimate love toward each one of us.

If we want to know what God is like, we look to Jesus who embodies kindness. Throughout the Gospels, we see Jesus expressing divine kindness to everyone, even those who appear to be undeserving. The only people Jesus publically called out were the church folk — the Scribes, Pharisees, Sadducees and the religious hypocrites. His kindness was so attractive that people came by the thousands to see Him at work and listen to His words. Wherever Jesus went, He always left people better off than when He found them.

Jesus showed us how *doing* is so much more important than *talking*; how *serving* is so much more important than *being served*. "The Son of Man did not come to be served but to serve" (Matthew 20:28). He showed us what true love and kindness looks like.

In 1 Corinthians 13, the Apostle Paul describes true

love:

Love is patient. Love is kind. It does not boast. It is not proud. — 1 Corinthians 13:4 (NIV)

Love is *kind*. That means love and kindness go together. You can't be kind while you're mugging people and expressing displeasure and impatience. I'm not saying that love has to always be grinning. There's a place for tough love. Sometimes love means confronting people about certain issues, but you can be kind even when you're confrontational. Your words and actions can come from a loving, caring place. Like a scholar-friend told me, "Don't confront people. Care-front them. Be care-frontational." So before you say a word, make sure you care about their body, mind, soul and spirit. Care about their well-being.

Jesus said:

"This is my commandment, that you love one another as I have loved you." — John 15:12

Every follower of Christ is called to show kindness toward others. Unfortunately, some people have the mistaken impression that kindness is an optional gift that goes to some people but not to others. That's not how it works. Kindness is not a gift like teaching or preaching or prophecy. Nobody can say they weren't given the gift of kindness because it's not a spiritual gift. God wants to cultivate each fruit, including kindness, in the lives of every Christian. Therefore, make kindness a regular fixture of your life.

A Word of Kindness at the Greatest Point of Need

Have you ever received a word of kindness that met you exactly at the point of need? Maybe it came at a time in your life when you desperately needed encouragement or affirmation. Other people might not have even known that you were hurting but God moved them to speak the right word to you at the right time. Maybe you were down in the dumps and hurting from being messed over. Then somebody came with a word of kindness and it made all the difference in the world.

The Bible tells a story about a woman who desperately needed the encouragement that Jesus provided:

A woman was there who had been subject to bleeding for twelve years. She had suffered a great deal under the care of many doctors and had spent all she had, yet instead of getting better she grew worse. When she heard about Jesus, she came up behind Him in the crowd and touched His cloak because she thought, "If I just touch His clothes, I will be healed." Immediately her bleeding stopped and she felt in her body that she was freed from her suffering.

At once Jesus realized that power had gone out from Him. He turned around in the crowd and asked, "Who touched my clothes?"

"You see the people crowding against you," His disciples answered, "and yet you can ask, 'Who touched me?'"

But Jesus kept looking around to see who had done it. Then the woman, knowing what had happened to her,

141

came and fell at His feet and, trembling with fear, told Him the whole truth. He said to her, "Daughter, your faith has healed you. Go in peace and be freed from your suffering." — Mark 5:25-34 (NIV)

For 12 long years, this woman had a hemorrhaging condition that couldn't be solved by physicians. The Bible says she "spent all she had" and worse, she "suffered a great deal" under these doctors. Their useless treatments caused her a lot of pain and left her completely broke. If that's not bad enough, this flow of blood made her unclean according to Jewish ceremonial law. These laws forced her to remain secluded because if she touched someone, they too would become unclean. She was forbidden from being in public, so for 12 years she was an outcast.

Obviously, this woman was desperate. For 12 years, she had been physically messed up. She was broke. She was in pain. She was ostracized from community. She was hurting and alone. So out of desperation, this woman came up with a plan.

When she heard about Jesus, she came up behind Him in the crowd and touched His cloak.

Wait a minute!

She snuck up from behind. She knew she was violating the Jewish laws and that she could get in big trouble for being out in public, and yet here she was. She told herself, "I can stay hidden. I don't need a face-to-face appointment with Jesus. I'm not calling His secretary. I don't want to cause any trouble here. I won't stand up in front of Him where I could accidentally touch Him and make Him unclean. But I don't need to. He has enough healing that if I get down low and touch the hem of His garment, I'll be healed. Nobody will even know I was here."

So she intentionally came up behind him, frail and anemic after more than a decade of hemorrhaging. And when she touched His robe, immediately she felt in her body that she was healed of the affliction. That humble act of faith accomplished more than all her money and 12 years of suffering under doctors could do. Then what happened?

Jesus realized that power had gone out from Him. He turned around in the crowd and asked, "Who touched my clothes?"

Jesus can always attract a crowd of people. It still happens today, but not everybody in the crowd wants the power of God. Not everybody wants to be humble at His feet. All some folk want is a selfie with Jesus. They are autograph-seekers, picture-takers who want their uncle, who doesn't even know how to work the camera, to take a quick pic. They want to show their friends on social media that they were with Jesus. But Jesus was tuned into the fact that this woman was acting in faith for a very specific healing. So in the middle of this crowd, He called her out.

One of the disciples — most likely Peter — told Jesus He was crazy to ask who had touched Him because there were so many people crowding up against Him. But Jesus persisted. He "kept looking around to see who had done it."

Finally, the woman came forward and fell at His feet

and confessed what she had done. The Bible says she was trembling with fear, but she probably had some joy as well because she had received what she came for. She got her healing.

Now look at what Jesus said to this woman who was fearfully trembling at His feet, having suffered beyond imagination and been an outcast from Jewish society for the past 12 years. I'd like to focus on just one word of Jesus ... the very first word that came out of His mouth. He said:

Daughter.

With this one powerful word, Jesus was practicing the ministry of kindness and compassion.

Daughter.

In a single word, Jesus was saying, "It's been many years since anyone reached out to you and embraced you. It's been too long since anyone accepted you and held you and treated you like a daughter. These people don't want to be close to you, but I do. You are being pushed away and abandoned by so many people, but not by me. Come into my embrace, daughter. You are loved and accepted, daughter. I do not rebuke you. Your faith has made you well. Now go in peace and be free."

This is the only woman in the Bible who received the honor of being called "daughter" by Jesus.

The right word spoken in a timely fashion is one of the kindest things you can do. Sometimes there's not a lot you need to say. Learn from Jesus about using the right word at the right time.

Sometimes the best thing you can do is to give a word of kindness at the greatest point of need.

Someone you know is troubled or suffering. Reach out to them with a word of kindness. Someone you know feels as if they don't belong. They feel like an outsider, as if everyone else is on the inside but they're not. Don't just feel pity for them. Call them son or daughter and then treat them like one.

My daughter Alicia was working in children's ministry at our church when she met a girl who was not able to live with her biological parents. When she learned that Alicia was the daughter of the pastor and the first lady, she said, "No way! That's not fair!" She was really longing for family and belonging, so when Meredith and I heard about it, we met with her one Sunday afternoon. She didn't have any godparents, so after talking with her awhile, we asked, "Would it be okay if we became your god-mom and god-dad?"

Her eyes grew wide and her face started to beam. It was as if we were making an offer that was too good to be true.

"We would love for you to be our god-daughter. We'll try to be the best god-parents that we can be. Would that be okay with you?"

She didn't say a word, but a smile broke out from ear to ear. She didn't have to say "yes" because it was written all over her face.

One of the things I've done for her was to put a candy jar with her name on it on my desk, fill it with her favorite candies and let her come into her god-dad's office after children's church, reach right in and get whatever she wanted. And I told her, "You can even bring one or two of your friends who have been good and respectful in children's church. Bring them with you and let them enjoy some of your candy as well."

Kindness matters. Nobody is exempt from being kind. You don't need a big house, special talents or a lot of money to be kind. All you need is a loving heart. Even if people have significant needs, like the woman who had been hemorrhaging for 12 years, you can still bless them with kindness. That woman needed Jesus' word of encouragement as much or more than she needed healing.

Daughter.

Like so many people today, this woman needed to belong. Jesus was saying, "You're my daughter. Now if you have any future needs, come back to me. I've got your back."

If we as God's people can learn to express this kind of kindness to people today, our communities will be completely transformed by the love of God.

Jesus Came to Show us Kindness

Jesus came to show us kindness. If we want to know what kindness looks like, look to Jesus. That's where we can find God's benevolence in action.

One amazing example of Jesus' kindness is found in the story of the woman who was caught in the act of adultery:

Now early in the morning He came again into the temple and all the people came to Him; and He sat down and taught them. Then the scribes and Pharisees brought to Him a woman caught in adultery. And when they had set her in the midst, they said to Him, "Teacher, this woman was caught in adultery, in the very act. Now Moses, in the law, commanded us that such should be stoned. But what do you say?" This they said, testing Him, that they might have something of which to accuse Him. But Jesus stooped down and wrote on the ground with His finger, as though He did not hear.

So when they continued asking Him, He raised Himself up and said to them, "He who is without sin among you, let him throw a stone at her first." And again He stooped down and wrote on the ground. Then those who heard it, being convicted by their conscience, went out one by one, beginning with the oldest even to the last. And Jesus was left alone and the woman standing in the midst. When Jesus had raised Himself up and saw no one but the woman, He said to her, "Woman, where are those accusers of yours? Has no one condemned you?"

She said, "No one, sir." And Jesus said to her, "Neither do I condemn you; go and sin no more." — John 8:2-11

Stop and think for a moment about what happened before they brought this woman to Jesus. One of these hypocrites was intentionally peeping through a window and caught her in the act of adultery. So when they brought her out, Jesus could have said, "So for what purpose were y'all spending your time looking in that window?" But He didn't say that. Some things never change. Even today, some people would rather point out other folks' messes than their own.

The Bible says that the religious leaders did this as a test to trap Jesus. They knew that if she was convicted of breaking the law of Moses, she should be stoned. Even worse, they had the audacity to test Jesus by twisting the words of Moses. Everybody knows it takes more than one to commit adultery. The law didn't say that if a couple is committing adultery, you should grab the woman and stone her. It said *adulterers*. Which begs the question: *Where was the guy? And was he one of those who brought the accusation?*

Regardless of these errors, Jesus didn't try to correct their theology. He ignored that and said to Himself, "Okay, if they want to have a stoning today, then can have a stoning. But first, I need to give them the ground rules."

Then Jesus started writing in the ground. After doing that for a while, He straightened up and said, "Let any one of you who is without sin be the first to throw a stone at her." It's significant to note that He didn't mention adultery or any certain brand of sin. He said "without sin." In other words, He was reminding them of the statutes. They knew that to be guilty of one sin meant to be guilty across the board. They knew God demanded perfection and not one of them could rise to that standard.

A lot of people do with sin what retired talk show host

David Letterman did for decades, i.e., create Top Ten Lists. They say, "I thank God I'm not like all those sinners who do the worst sins." No! Jesus put everyone on a level playing field. He showed how all people are sinners and equally in need of God's grace and forgiveness.

On this occasion, Jesus scribbled in the dirt. We don't know what He was writing, but I suspect it might have been something like, "Jericho Hilton, Room 34." "Last year's tax form number CMCXVII." "The promise you made to Brutus that you had no intention of fulfilling." Whatever He wrote, it was like arrows shot straight to the heart of the men who were watching Him write. We know that because the accusers began to leave, from the oldest (who had sinned the most) to the youngest.

Then when all of the accusers were gone, Jesus looked up at the woman and asked, "Is nobody here to condemn you?"

"Nobody, sir," she said. "They're all gone."

Then Jesus said, "Neither do I condemn you."

Wait a minute. The Christian faith has a lot to say about holiness. From a very early age, we are taught that our faith is expressed through proper action. And here we see Jesus face to face with an adulterer and the first thing He does is free her from condemnation.

We as moral Christians are tempted constantly to condemn people but that's not God's way. We know this from the oft-quoted Bible verse that reads:

For God so loved the world that He gave His only begotten Son, that whoever believes in Him should not perish but have everlasting life. For God did not send His Son into the world to condemn the world, but that the world through Him might be saved. — John 3:16-17

Jesus didn't come to condemn anyone. He never consigned anyone to hell, saying, "That one's a hopeless cause." No! Some church folk get their kicks showing up at parades with signs telling folk why they're going to hell and how hot the flames will be when they get there. That does not come from the heart of God, who assured us He did not send Jesus to condemn the world.

"Neither do I condemn you," says Jesus. "I'm freeing you to live a better life. I won't condemn you for the life you are leaving behind. That's not you anymore. You are free from all that. Go and sin no more. You are free to live a much better life now."

In the Sermon on the Mount, Jesus called us to be salt and light to the world (Matthew 5:13-16). That means we need to stop condemning people and instead show them a better way. That's the fruit of kindness in action.

The Kind Samaritan

Jesus told a story in Luke 10 that has in time become known as the story of the Good Samaritan. This is an unfortunate title, because the word "good" implies that this man was morally upright, when in fact Luke says nothing of the kind. Samaritans in general had a negative reputation. They were seen as half-breeds — Jews who had intermarried with pagans — and the name "Samaritan" had a racist connotation in that culture. No Jew would ever call a Samaritan "good."

I prefer to call him the Kind Samaritan. Here's how Jesus told that story:

> *Then Jesus answered and said: "A certain man went down from Jerusalem to Jericho and fell among thieves, who stripped him of his clothing, wounded him and departed, leaving him half dead. Now by chance a certain priest came down that road. And when he saw him, he passed by on the other side. Likewise a Levite, when he arrived at the place, came and looked and passed by on the other side. But a certain Samaritan, as he journeyed, came where he was. And when he saw him, he had compassion. So he went to him and bandaged his wounds, pouring on oil and wine; and he set him on his own animal, brought him to an inn and took care of him. On the next day, when he departed, he took out two denarii, gave them to the innkeeper and said to him, 'Take care of him; and whatever more you spend, when I come again, I will repay you.' So which of these three do you think was neighbor to him who fell among the thieves?"*
>
> *And he said, "He who showed mercy on him."*
>
> *Then Jesus said to him, "Go and do likewise."* — Luke 10:30-37

Notice how it says a priest "happened to be going down the same road." We view life's circumstances as if they happen by chance, but Jesus was showing how it wasn't chance at all. In reality, life is one test after another. Situations will arise that challenge our priorities and outlook on life. Jesus was specifically showing us how some encounters look as if they happen by chance, and yet they turn out to be the perfect challenge to our core beliefs. In this case, the priest is a holy man who was supposed to embody God's most sacred qualities, and yet he proved that he was without kindness and compassion. He ignored the injured man and passed by on the other side of the road.

Then along came a Levite. Levites were church men. They were in the choir. They were ushers and elders. They did hands-on ministry at the temple. But the Levite acted just like the priest, passing by on the other side. Jesus was showing how it's possible to be religious and claim to be holy and yet know nothing whatsoever about God's core quality of kindness. In fact, we know these men lacked holiness because they lacked kindness.

These church men who "happened to be going down the same road" prove that you don't have to go out of your way to find people to help. God will put them in your way. When you least expect it — when you have plenty of reasons why not to stop — you will look up and see them in your path. You might think it's chance, but God says, "No, I trust you enough to put you on the same road. Now go and show them my kindness."

The only person who expressed the fruit of compassion in this story was a social outcast, the Samaritan. He was an illegitimate half-breed. He would not have been familiar with the Jewish religion and laws, and yet he possessed a depth of compassionate that the religious men lacked. They may have felt bad about the injured man in the ditch but they did nothing to demonstrate their pity.

Don't be someone who feels bad about the pain of the world but does nothing about it. Hurting people will see your broken heart and say, "Thanks a lot but your pity does absolutely nothing to relieve my suffering." The world doesn't need your broken heart. We already saw how kindness is not just talk. To be authentic, kindness is felt through loving acts of compassion.

See how the Samaritan expressed the fruit of kindness by pouring oil and wine on the wounds and bandaging them. Then he put the man on his animal and took him to a safe place where he would be well-cared for. The next day he gave money and instructions to the innkeeper before departing on business of his own. Notice how his kindness didn't tie him down forever. He performed a wonderful act of benevolence and then said "Bye."

When you are compassionate and kind, you can still live your life. Like the Samaritan, you can be intentional about sharing the burden with other people in ministry. You don't have to do it all yourself.

Every church should foster a network of kindness. Some people may be gifted in starting a ministry and others in finishing it. Many ministries can't be done alone. Partners need to stand together in kindness. Nobody has to be alone if everyone is doing their part within their sphere of ministry. These spheres will overlap as each person expresses kindness and compassion to those who are closest to them.

One area of great need is among single parents who are bearing a heavy burden, trying their best to "do it all" for their kids. Friends and family ought to be kind and give them a break sometimes. Another group is the sick and elderly who are experiencing emotional trauma or financial hardship. If we open our eyes, we will see the injured people lying beside the highway.

You may be traveling fast down the highway of life, but pull over and find someone to help. Spend a few hours a week with that lonely grandmother or grandfather. Take that boy or girl out for their favorite meal. Run errands and go shopping for someone who needs it. Bless someone with your intentional acts of kindness.

In the Lord's Prayer, we pray that God's kingdom will come. How will His kingdom come if we don't express kindness? We change people's lives for all eternity by just being there for them. We transform our cities and neighborhoods by showing a little kindness. People will stop and notice, saying, "Those folk sure are kind. They even look more attractive than the average person. What do they have that I don't have?"

That's when you tell them about this delicious cluster of fruit that grows plump and sweet with love, joy, peace, longsuffering and kindness. Expect miracles like this to happen when you cultivate these priceless, eternal treasures in your life.

Abide in the Lord and you will bear much fruit!

Goodness

*But the fruit of the
Spirit is love, joy, peace,
longsuffering, kindness,
goodness, faithfulness,
gentleness and self-control.
–Galatians 5.22-23a*

The sixth fruit of the Spirit mentioned in Galatians 5 is goodness.

What is goodness? **Goodness is openhearted generosity toward others, above what we think they deserve.**

Goodness means being generous to others, even when we think they don't deserve it. It means being openhearted. Goodness may sound very similar to kindness and it is. Our working definition for kindness is *benevolence in action*. You might think of kindness and goodness as siblings. They're related. They have many of the same inherent tendencies. The main difference is that kindness is reflected more in action, while goodness goes to the heart of the matter. Kindness is benevolence in action, but it's important to know that you can display acts of kindness that come from a heart that is not necessarily good.

It is possible to appear to be kind but not be necessarily good.

God designed these fruits to be complimentary. As we develop each fruit in our lives, all of the gaps will be filled. He wants us to have both of these siblings in generous measure. He wants our kindness to be expressed from a heart of goodness. When people see how openhearted and generous we are, they will see the authentic goodness of God in our heart. Our goodness will display the true nature of God to the world.

Imitating our Good, Good Father

What does it mean to display the nature of God? To answer this question, we need to understand *first and foremost* that God is good. He gives us the fruit of goodness because He is making us more like Himself. We are his people. We are the sheep of His pasture. When we go out into the world, we ought to resemble our Daddy.

When a child doesn't look anything like his or her parents, it gets people wondering. When they grow up and act in ways that dishonor the parents, it reflects badly on the family name. The fruit of the Spirit improves our family resemblance. People will see our goodness and say, "Ah … that reflects well on their Father. Now I can see that the Lord is very good."

God doesn't merely do good things. *He is good.* The same is true with the fruit of love. We know that *God is love.* That doesn't mean God *has a lot* of love. It means He literally *is love.*

Love is the essence of who God is.

Similarly, the Bible speaks of God as good. He doesn't just do good things. He is good through and through.

Goodness is the essence of who God is.

The Bible is filled with passages reminding us that God is good:

Enter His gates with thanksgiving and His courts with praise; give thanks to Him and praise His name. For the Lord is good and His love endures forever; His faithfulness continues through all generations. — Psalm 100:4-5

Oh, give thanks to the Lord, for He is good. For His mercy endures forever. — Psalm 106:1b

Oh, give thanks to the Lord, for He is good. For His mercy endures forever. — Psalm 136:1

The Lord doesn't just do good things. He literally is good.

Sometimes when God's people are going through troubles, the enemy comes and whispers, "If God was good, He wouldn't let you go through this hardship. God can't be good."

That's the voice of a liar. That is Satan attacking the very character of God's goodness. If you ever hear that from the enemy, say, "That's a lie because God is good. I trust that He knows what is best for me. He is so good that He cannot cause anything bad to happen. Even if I walk through the valley of the shadow of death, I will fear no evil because the Lord is with me. His plan is to strengthen me and bring me through to the other side."

You may feel as if you're walking through the valley of the shadow of death that David described in Psalm 23, but never forget who is there with you. Fear not! His rod and His staff will comfort you. He will not abandon you. You may not like the setting but you will like your companion. You're in good company. If you're in a bad place, don't invest in real estate there. Keep on moving. You are passing through to a better place where God has prepared a table of blessings in the presence of your enemies. With God, you will overcome.

Know that you are going to a good place because you are traveling with a good God.

Let's see what Jesus said about the goodness of God:

As Jesus started on His way, a man ran up to Him and fell on his knees before Him. "Good teacher," he asked, "what must I do to inherit eternal life?"

"Why do you call me good?" Jesus answered. "No one is good — except God alone." — Mark 10:17-18 (NIV)

Here we see Jesus — who is God — declaring that no one is good except God alone. Goodness is the essence of who He is. Scripture is so adamant about God's goodness that we should never question that fact. When the circumstances are lousy, don't blame God. The thief comes to kill, steal and destroy (John 10:10), so blame it on him. Blame it on Satan but don't blame it on our good God.

Satan leads you into bad circumstances but God can lead you out.

Contrary to what we might think, our good God promised that we would go through tough circumstances. Scripture never said that every day would be easy and happy. Folk like to claim the promises of God that relate to happiness and prosperity, but they forget the promises about going through trials. Jesus said, "In this world you will have tribulation" (John 16:33). We are told not to be surprised when ordeals come, as if it's strange (1 Peter 4:12). We are told not to be surprised when the world hates us (1 John 3:13). We are told to bless those who persecute us (Romans 12:14). Those are only a few of the many scriptures that assure us we will go through tribulation. And yet our good God promised to bring us through each trouble to a greater joy on the other side.

People are tempted to believe that if they're living right, everything should be going good. They expect good things to happen to good people and bad things to happen to bad people. And yet nothing could be further from the truth! You can be dead-center in the will of God and experience all hell breaking loose, while your heathen friends are living in comfort and happiness. And you wonder, "Wait a minute. How can this be? Why am I trudging through hell while they're sipping cool drinks and relaxing in their beach chairs?"

The Psalms provide us with answers to this troubling question. We have already seen how the Lord promises to walk with us even in the valley of the shadow of death, to a prepared place in the presence of our enemies (Psalm 23). Another powerful word of encouragement comes from Psalms 37:

> *Do not fret because of those who are evil or be envious of those who do wrong; for like the grass they will soon wither, like green plants they will soon die away. Trust in the Lord and do good; dwell in the land and enjoy safe pasture. Take delight in the Lord and He will give you the desires of your heart.*
>
> *Commit your way to the Lord; trust in Him and He will do this: He will make your righteous reward shine like the dawn, your vindication like the noonday sun. Be still before the Lord and wait patiently for Him; do not fret when people succeed in their ways, when they carry out their wicked schemes.*
>
> *Refrain from anger and turn from wrath; do not fret; It leads only to evil. For those who are evil will be destroyed, but those who hope in the Lord will inherit the land. A little while and the wicked will be no more; though you look for them, they will not be found. But the meek will inherit the land and enjoy peace and prosperity.* — Psalm 37 (NIV)

Do not fret when the wicked succeed in their schemes. It's only temporary. In a little while you will be blessed. Do not fret!

It's okay to say, "I don't like what I'm going through now," but don't stop there. Keep moving! Declare, "I don't like it but I serve a good God. My good, good Father will bring me through to a better place. My circumstances may be uncertain but God's goodness is unshakeable. I stand on the solid rock of God's goodness!"

The Lord has you covered. Delight in Him and He will give you the desires of your heart. And if your desires are not in line with His purpose, He will shift them toward goodness as you abide in Him. Delight in God's goodness, which will never fail.

Goodness through Deliberate Action

We began this chapter by explaining that goodness is openheartedness and generosity toward others, above what we think they deserve. Let's build upon that definition by understanding this truth:

Goodness is most valuable when it is displayed through deliberate action.

Speaking to the Pharisees, Jesus said:

"A good man out of the good treasure of his heart brings forth good things …" — Matthew 12:35

Good men and women are those in whom God is developing the character of goodness. Out of these good people, God brings forth good things that come from the treasure of their heart. This goodness will be obvious to everyone. This is what it means to display goodness through deliberate actions.

Don't just talk about God. Don't just sing and shout words of praise without demonstrating deliberate actions of goodness. Let the evidence of your goodness be obvious to everyone. Like the great "theologian" Janet Jackson once asked, "What have you done for me lately?"[11] Show your love for God through your acts of goodness. Goodness is not worth much if it stays in your heart, but it is extremely valuable when it's on display.

A good man out of the good treasure of his heart brings forth good things.

The world won't be blessed by what's inside your heart. People will only be blessed by what comes forth from the good treasure of your heart, so get it out. Put it on your face. Put it in your hands. Put it in your feet. Walk somewhere and use your hands to make life better for someone. Get it out of your heart and put it on display for the world to see.

God worked some good things in you. It's up to you to work them out. Earlier in this study, we read this scripture which also applies here:

For we are His workmanship, created in Christ Jesus for good works, which God prepared beforehand that we should walk in them. — Ephesians 2:10

The verses preceding verse 10 say that we are saved by grace through faith. Salvation is a gift of God, not of works, so that nobody can boast. Verse 10 is all about purpose. God created us for the purpose of fulfilling the good works that He prepared for us to do. God created you and me to do good works. This is our purpose so don't miss it. Walk it out.

---

[11] "What have you Done for me Lately?" by Janet Jackson, James Harris III and Terry Lewis (A&M Records, 1985).

Don't leave the planet with your works undone. You have no business dying until you have worked out the good works that brought you here in the first place. Unfortunately, the cemetery is one of the richest places in the world, with all the unspent treasure buried there. Too many people went to the grave before doing what they were built to do. They died without letting that good treasure out of their hearts.

God called us to do good works. That's why the fruit of the Spirit is goodness. God put good things in us. He is developing and cultivating even more goodness in us today. Our job is to get that goodness out.

What good things are you doing for others? You are here to make a difference for other people. You are God's workmanship, created in Christ Jesus for good works. The fruit of your goodness is displayed through deliberate action, so learn to imitate your good, good Father.

The A-B-Cs of Discovering God's Purpose

Since God has a specific purpose for you on earth, which includes good works for you to accomplish, the question is this: How do you discover your purpose? To answer that, let's take a moment to review what I call the A-B-Cs of Discovering God's purpose:

A — Ask.

Jesus said, "Ask and you will receive" (Matthew 7:7). If you want to know your purpose, just ask. God will show you why He brought you here. Pray until you receive an answer. Say, "Lord, why do you have me here?" Then

163

don't check out. Keep your eyes open and watch for an answer.

B — Observe your Burdens.

After asking, observe the ways in which God is speaking to you about your purpose. The first things to observe are the burdens of your heart. What in your heart are you most concerned about? You may have a passion to eliminate suffering or to see that someone gets justice. We see that kind of a burden in the heart of Nehemiah, who lived at a time in the Old Testament when the city of Jerusalem was in ruins. His heart was burdened because his people, the Jews, were vulnerable to their enemies. So he got an extended leave of absence from his boss, the King of Persia, to go and rebuild the walls of Jerusalem.

Your burdens are a clue to something you're supposed to do. It doesn't matter if you're still in school or retired. At any stage in life, know that you are working for the King. Say, "Lord, where am I supposed to go? Who am I supposed to minister to? How can I help?"

Maybe you have a passion to help someone in need. Maybe you know someone who's hungry, incarcerated or having trouble making ends meet. Maybe you want to come alongside a young, struggling single parent and let your home be a safe place for the kids. It takes a village to raise a child and that's not a political statement. It's a fact of life. Many of us grew up in a world where the neighbors knew who all the kids were and what time they were supposed to be home. Personally, I remember Mrs. Burgess next door being my second mama, making sure I was alright, especially if my mom was tied up somewhere else. It's more complicated in an age where everybody's working and it's hard to find good daycare. That's why we need folk in the body of Christ to exercise their gifts for helping other parents.

Observe your burdens. Your heart will tell you what God has created you to do to help others.

C — Confer with Others.

To discover God's purpose in your life, confer with others. Have any words of guidance or affirmation been prayed over you? God often uses people to speak His will into your life. Ask God to speak to you through people you know and trust. You'll know if it's something God wants you to do. Confer with others.

D — Dreams.

Look at the dreams of your heart, especially those that are unfilled. Just because you're getting older doesn't mean it's too late or that all your dreams have been realized. Pray that God will awaken the important ones that are still to be fulfilled. If you're older, you might have a bucket list but don't stop there. Have a dream list. Make a list of things you'd still like to see God do through you to bless others. Don't let those dreams get neglected! If it is God's plan to fulfill those dreams, you will be amazed to see Him bring that work to completion.

E — Exposure and Experience.

To complete His good work in you, God is exposing

you to people who need your good works. He is exposing you to divine opportunities and open doors. He has also given you important experiences. The experiences you've had are often indications of where God wants you to go in the future. You have been faithful in small things and so He wants to give you greater experiences. Your experience also qualifies you to come alongside others and help them develop their gifts and callings. It enables you to encourage others who are going through similar hardships as you have experienced. God is calling you to share your experiences with others and say, "I know what that's like. I've been there. Let me help you walk through this difficult season."

F — Faith.

For a clearer picture of God's purpose and calling, be a faith-walking person. Don't be timid and afraid to exercise your gifts. Be like Caleb, who was one of 12 spies who went to survey the Promised Land under Moses' direction (Numbers 13). When they returned from spying out the land, ten spies spoke in fear about the giants in Canaan's walled cities. Only Caleb and Joshua said, "We can do this! God is more than strong enough to help us succeed." Caleb was 40 years old when he was full of faith, ready to take the Promised Land. Unfortunately, nearly the whole nation of Israel became infected with the unbelief of the unfaithful spies. As a result, God sent that entire generation back out into the wilderness to die. Only Joshua, Caleb and the children were allowed to live another 40 years and go into the Promised Land. Soon after that, Caleb declared, "I'm 85 years old and I'm still as strong as I was when I was 40" (Joshua 14:6-14).

Even if your body needs a little help, your spirit can be strong. Your faith can be strong. Be a faith-walking person so that the good treasures stored in your heart will be able to come forth and bless others.

<u>G — Gifts.</u>

If you want to know what God wants to get *out* of you, look at what He put *into* you! He has made investments in your life, and He wants a return on those investments, including your spiritual gifts, your natural abilities, and your learned skills. These are resources you can and should use to bring glory to God and to benefit the people He brings into your life.

To review, the A-B-Cs of discovering God's purpose are:

A — Ask,
B — Observe your Burdens,
C — Confer with Others,
D — Dreams,
E — Exposure/Experience,
F — Faith, and
G — Gifts.

Examples of Goodness in Action

In this section I'll share a few examples of goodness in action from scripture. The first example is from the Apostle Barnabas. He wasn't one of the 12 disciples, but the New Testament refers to him as an apostle because that title wasn't limited to Jesus' disciples. In fact, one of the disciples, Judas, betrayed Jesus and committed suicide, but that didn't catch God off guard. He already had a replacement in mind and that was Saul, who was renamed Paul. But others in addition to the 12 disciples received the special title of apostle, and Barnabas was one of them.

This is what Acts 11 says about Barnabas:

The Lord's hand was with [the church in Antioch] and a great number of people believed and turned to the Lord. News of this reached the church in Jerusalem and they sent Barnabas to Antioch. When he arrived and saw what the grace of God had done, he was glad and encouraged them all to remain true to the Lord with all their hearts. He was a good man, full of the Holy Spirit and faith and a great number of people were brought to the Lord. Then Barnabas went to Tarsus to look for Saul and when he found him, he brought him to Antioch. So for a whole year Barnabas and Saul met with the church and taught great numbers of people. The disciples were called Christians first at Antioch. — Acts 11:21-26*

Notice what verse 23 said about Barnabas: "He was a good man, full of the Holy Spirit and faith and a great number of people were brought to the Lord." The church in Jerusalem sent Barnabas because of his character. He had the fruit of goodness. He didn't have "issues" that were boiling just under the surface. He was a good man, full of the Holy Spirit and faith. This was especially important as they saw gentiles learning about Jesus and wanting to be saved. Bringing non-Jewish people into this new church was a completely foreign idea for the early believers. So they brought Barnabas because they knew they could trust him.

Each one of us should yearn for the qualities that Barnabas possessed. We should pray, "Lord, make me a Barnabas. I want to be known as a good person. I want to be full of the Holy Ghost and full of faith. When people mention my name, let them say, 'That's a good man. That's a good woman.'"

It's not enough to be known for being filled with the Holy Spirit or for having faith. The fruit of that faith needs to be displayed with intentional acts of goodness. Ask God to help you cultivate the fruit of goodness so that when people think of you, they won't think of somebody with issues, with an axe to grind, who has a sharp edge. You won't be known for goodness if you allow those kinds of attitudes to remain in your life.

Goodness is openhearted generosity toward others, above what we think they deserve.

Notice how Barnabas left Antioch, traveled to Tarsus and brought Saul back with him. This was not long after Saul's conversion, when a lot of Christians would have mistrusted Saul because he had been one of their worst persecutors. Why do you suppose Barnabas pursued Saul?

To answer that question, we need to go back to Acts 9 and the conversion of Saul. After God blinded Saul on the road to Damascus, God spoke to a man named Ananias and told him to go and speak to Saul. But naturally Ananias had some concerns, based on Saul's reputation.

Then Ananias answered, "Lord, I have heard from many about this man, how much harm he has done to

Your saints in Jerusalem. And here he has authority from the chief priests to bind all who call on Your name." But the Lord said to him, "Go, for he is a chosen vessel of mine to bear my name before Gentiles, kings and the children of Israel." — Acts 9:13-15

God said, "This man is my chosen instrument to proclaim my name to the Gentiles." In time, the word got out that God had chosen this former persecutor to have a special calling to minister to non-Jewish people. Barnabas knew this and so he went to get Saul, even though Barnabas was more than qualified and even though Saul was not as mature as he. Barnabas wanted to set Saul up for success, so he brought him to minister with him in Antioch.

Now that's goodness! Barnabas was not like some people who set others up to fail, then brag, "I knew he wouldn't be able to succeed." If you are good, you will do all you can to help people succeed. So pray that God will give you a good spirit like Barnabas.

Look how for a whole year Barnabas and Saul taught great numbers of people in Antioch. You would have thought the Jewish followers of Christ would have first been called Christians in Jerusalem, but they weren't. They were first called Christians here in Antioch where Barnabas was working. Here we see God working most fervently in a distant place, among people who were not even Jews. God was still blessing the apostles in Jerusalem, but He was drawing their attention to a movement that was taking them out of their comfort zone.

God still works like that today. If you want to know the

heart of God, look at where He's moving. It won't always be where you expect or where you are most comfortable. And don't expect God to move like He did when you were younger. Older Christians are sometimes concerned when they see revival breaking out among young folks. They're uncomfortable with all these new kinds of music and culture and tattoos and piercings. It's time to get up off of them! Of course they look and act different than you. If God's hand is on them, leave them alone! And celebrate them! Give them space to grow. If they don't connect with the older people's church, give them their own service with their own music.

In other words, don't throw a fit because church isn't how you want it to be. It's not all about you, boo! Church is about other people who are all different from each other. Learn from Barnabas, who went out of his way to bring in Saul, the young blood, to set him up to succeed. Learn from the Jewish church in Jerusalem, who endorsed these edgy happenings among Gentiles in Antioch. Saul went on to become the Apostle Paul. He wrote two-thirds of the Epistles and was one of the most influential Christians in history, but he might not have been able to do it without the support of a good man named Barnabas.

Another example of goodness in action comes from Acts 15. This is a continuation of the story of Barnabas and Saul, who is now called Paul. They had returned to Antioch, after a few years of traveling together and establishing new churches in Asia Minor.

Then after some days Paul said to Barnabas, "Let us now go back and visit our brethren in every city where we have preached the word of the Lord and see how they are doing." Now Barnabas was determined to take with them John called Mark. But Paul insisted that they should not take with them the one who had departed from them in Pamphylia and had not gone with them to the work. Then the contention became so sharp that they parted from one another. And so Barnabas took Mark and sailed to Cyprus; but Paul chose Silas and departed, being commended by the brethren to the grace of God. — Acts 15:36-40

So Paul told Barnabas, "Let's take another trip and visit the believers in all the towns where we traveled." Barnabas thought that was a great idea and so he got ready to contact John Mark, who had done some ministry with them earlier. But Paul wouldn't have it. He said, "No way. When things got rough and when people who hate Jesus threatened to harm us, John Mark deserted us. He got scared and left us hanging."

We know that John Mark's mother had a church in her home in Jerusalem, so maybe John Mark was familiar with comfortable church, with happy saints singing and praying and eating chicken. Then when things got rough out on the frontier, he ran back home to his mama. In Acts 15, Barnabas was saying, "Give him a chance! It was his first time under pressure. Sure, he wimped out once but he'll never learn if you don't give him a second chance."

But Paul wouldn't have it. He only wanted first-string players to take into battle. In fact, the Bible says that Paul and Barnabas had such a sharp contention about John Mark that they parted company. Paul found a new guy named

Silas to travel with, while Barnabas traveled with John Mark. We know that Paul eventually got over all objections to John Mark, because years later, Paul commended him to Timothy, telling Timothy to "Get Mark and bring him with you, because he is helpful to me in my ministry" (2 Timothy 4:11).

Barnabas was such a good man that he couldn't leave John Mark on the sidelines. His desire to set up John Mark for success was so great that he withstood the very vocal protestations of the Apostle Paul. When Paul wrote off John Mark as a lost cause, Barnabas helped him mature enough to eventually write the Gospel of Mark.

Imagine practicing that kind of goodness in your life today. Imagine being so sensitive to someone's need to be discipled that nothing will stand in the way of you helping them. That is the kind of goodness practiced by Barnabas. Every now and then you have to be willing to stand your ground against somebody who's more strong and vocal and pushy. Sometimes you need to assert stubbornness to allow goodness to win out.

Paul and Barnabas had very different temperaments and that's okay. God created all different kinds of people with different niches to fill. The most important thing to remember — no matter your temperament — is to cultivate the fruit of goodness in your heart and allow that goodness to express itself in acts of love for the people around you.

The life of the Apostle Barnabas displays several wonderful examples of goodness in action. So does the life of David, who made a simple declaration of goodness in the Shepherd's Psalm:

Surely goodness and mercy shall follow me all the days of my life and I will dwell in the house of the Lord forever. — Psalm 23:6

David said, "Surely, goodness and mercy shall follow me." That declaration was literally fulfilled throughout the life of David, from start to finish. He acted in goodness when everything was going well. He acted in goodness when his world was falling apart. We see that goodness long before David became king, when he was just a little shepherd boy. He heard about how Goliath, the Philistine army's champion, had the Israelite army paralyzed with fear. Then David found the boldness to take his sling and a few pebbles from a streambed and meet that giant head-on saying, "You come against me with sword and spear and javelin, but I come against you in the name of the Lord Almighty" (1 Samuel 17:45).

As you probably know, David brought down that giant with one stone flung from his shepherd's sling. Now look what happened next, after David went to meet with King Saul:

Now when he had finished speaking to Saul, the soul of Jonathan was knit to the soul of David and Jonathan loved him as his own soul. Saul took him that day and would not let him go home to his father's house anymore. Then Jonathan and David made a covenant, because he loved him as his own soul. And Jonathan took off the robe that was on him and gave it to David, with his armor, even to his sword and his bow and his belt. — 1 Samuel 18:1-4

Wait a minute! Here we see Jonathan, who is the heir to the throne, taking off his robe and his armor and giving it to David. Why would a prince with such a powerful inheritance take his armor and his robe, which was symbolic of power, and give it to a shepherd boy? David has no connection with royalty. His only experience was with dirty sheep. He hung out with them day and night. Why would Jonathan do something as crazy as this?

First, because God's hand was on David.

Going back in time, God appointed the Prophet Samuel to anoint David, the least of all Jesse's children, to be the future king of Israel. Then God gave David the boldness and skill to conquer a mighty warrior that the Israelite army was afraid of. That got the attention of King Saul, who installed David in his palace so he could minister through music and his giftedness on the harp. That in turn led to the sacred covenant between Jonathan and David, despite the fact that Saul soon developed an intense hatred and fear of David.

Notice how God knit the hearts of Jonathan and David together. That speaks about a rare kind of relationships. You know what that's like if you ever said about someone, "From the first time we met, we had a commonality." Magnify that by several times and this is what Jonathan and David had. They were prepared to die for each other. It's as if they were an extension of each other's heart. I've heard secular people twist that and try to say it was an ungodly relationship but that's not what the Bible says. In the

Jewish culture, women could create soul ties with other women and men with men. Our culture is so out of touch with God's design for healthy relationships that we have a difficult time understanding healthy bonds that are not sexual.

So to return to the question, why would Jonathan be so willing to place his robe and his armor on this lowly shepherd boy David?

Because God put goodness in Jonathan's heart.

This is the kind of goodness that God wants to give us through the fruit of the Spirit. This is what goodness looks like. It means being willing to divest ourselves of anything in order to invest in somebody else. It means being generous with the things that are important to us. It means saying, "You need a robe. You need armor. No, we're not going down to the thrift store to see what we can find. Here. Take mine. You have some amazing things to do with these gifts I'm giving you."

Jonathan gave David his robe, his armor and his sword. This is what goodness looks like. David was able to be blessed with goodness because of the generosity of Jonathan.

Paying Goodness Forward

Pause for a moment to think about all those times when you were blessed with exceptional goodness. Maybe you had a childhood teacher or mentor who, like Barnabas, overlooked your failings or your lack of experience and led you into opportunities that positively shaped your life. More recently, you can probably name some good people who gave you a job or advice or helped get you to where you are today. For some reason, they said, "I'm going to invest in this young man or woman. I'm going to invest in this older person. I'm going to share God's goodness with them, whether they deserve it or not."

The question is: *How do you respond when someone blesses you with goodness?*

The Bible teaches us how to respond. We are taught to pay that goodness forward to someone else. Pay it forward, without looking for anything in return. When true goodness is given, it does not expect anything in return. Goodness is content to just be good. Therefore, make up your mind to be good simply *for goodness sake*. Be good because it's good to be good. It's right to be right. It is nice to be nice. Don't be like worldly folk who are looking at the profit margin and how much return they'll see on their investments.

Don't judge to see if others are worth your goodness. We have built all kinds of conditions and qualifications around goodness. The fact is, if we only gave goodness to folk who deserve it, nobody would ever get it. It would be so rare, you wouldn't even see it on the list of fruit in Galatians 5. Thankfully, God has given the fruit of the Spirit freely to everyone who will receive it, whether they deserve it or not. The Bible says that while we were His enemies, Christ died for us (Romans 5:8). God the Father was not up in heaven looking for worthy people, saying,

"Boy, I sure hope some of them meet my qualifications."

There's a movie called "Seven Pounds of Grace," in which the actor Will Smith performs some amazing acts of goodness for seven people, but it's not clear why he's doing it. Then as the storyline develops, we see that he is riddled with guilt because of his negligence that caused the death of seven people. He was using a cell phone while driving and he had a head-on collision that killed his girl and six others. That led him on a quest to find seven people who he considered to be worthy enough to receive his seven extraordinary acts of kindness. He even gave his life in order for the seventh person to live.

Years ago, while I was watching this movie, I said to myself, "Oh! This is the antithesis of what Jesus did. Will Smith's character went to great lengths to make sure that those who received his extraordinary gifts were worthy, while Jesus, on the other hand, gave His extraordinary gifts specifically to people who are not worthy."

In case you've forgotten, you and I are sitting here in grace *not* because we are worthy of salvation. We are sitting here in grace because we are unworthy of salvation. We couldn't do a thing about getting our lives together. And in our helplessness, Love came down from glory. Love hung on a cross. Love said, "Take my gift, even though you don't deserve it. Let me bless you with the fruit of goodness, simply because I delight in blessing you. And now that you've seen how grace and love and goodness are given, I send you out into the world to pay it forward. Don't look for worthy people, okay? Look for anyone who needs my love and my goodness and — whether you think they deserve it or not — give it to them."

Pay goodness forward.

Returning to 1 Samuel, we read about a ten year period when Saul was consumed with jealousy and hatred of David. His fear and jealousy drove him to send his army after David. During that time while David and his men were hiding in caves, Jonathan found him and tried to help him. The goodness in Jonathan's heart was too pure to allow him to abandon David, even at great risk to his own life. The Bible says:

> *David was in the Wilderness of Ziph in a forest. Then Jonathan, Saul's son, arose and went to David in the woods and strengthened his hand in God. And he said to him, "Do not fear, for the hand of Saul my father shall not find you. You shall be king over Israel and I shall be next to you. Even my father Saul knows that." So the two of them made a covenant before the Lord. And David stayed in the woods and Jonathan went to his own house. — 1 Samuel 23:15b-18*

This is amazing, to see the young man Jonathan, who was the rightful heir to the throne, encouraging David not to fear and even assuring him that he would be the next king of Israel. "And I will submit to you," he says.

That's goodness.

Jonathan would rather share God's goodness with his father's greatest enemy than receive power and treasure and fame by becoming the next king of Israel. He was strengthening David's hands in the Lord. He was encouraging David and letting him know he still had at least one friend who would never abandon him. When they parted, David's tears had dried. He was encouraged. He was stronger than when Jonathan found him out there in the wilderness.

That tells us something important about goodness, that goodness leaves folk in a better state than when you found them. If people are more jacked-up after you leave them, you can be sure that the wrong fruit is growing on your vine. That means it's time for pruning. Nurture the fruit of goodness in your life. That fruit allows you to leave everyone in a better place than when you found them. Even if you can't help them, you can bless them in small ways. You can share a smile or a word of encouragement with them. Even if everything they are doing seems to be counter to the will of God, you don't need to dig them deeper in that ditch.

When a rich young ruler asked Jesus how he could inherit eternal life, this was Jesus' response:

> *Then Jesus, looking at him, loved him and said to him, "One thing you lack: Go your way, sell whatever you have and give to the poor and you will have treasure in heaven; and come, take up the cross and follow me." But he was sad at this word and went away sorrowful, for he had great possessions.* — Mark 10:21-22

One thing that Jesus won't do is to help someone who doesn't want His help. So, when Jesus saw this man who had everything in the eyes of the world, He knew He couldn't help him. This interaction is extremely significant when you consider the things that Jesus *didn't say*. He didn't tell the man how messed up his priorities were. He didn't preach at him. He didn't condemn him.

Jesus looked at him and loved him.

Sure, you can give people help and advice if they ask for it. But more importantly, pour the universal gift of goodness into every human interaction. Follow the example of Jesus. Look at them and love them. Refuse to be a curse in anybody's life. Even when you can't do anything else, allow the goodness in your heart to bubble up and be a blessing.

Let's get back to the life of David, fast forwarding to a time when Saul is dead, Jonathan is dead and David has been king for many years. David's army subdued the enemies of Israel, which gave David room to reflect on God's goodness that was given to him by Jonathan.

Now David said, "Is there still anyone who is left of the house of Saul, that I may show him kindness for Jonathan's sake?" — 2 Samuel 9:1

David wants to pay it forward. Long after Jonathan is gone, David is still saying, "Can I pay it forward in any other way, above and beyond what I did when he was alive? I still remember the covenant I made with him. I still remember when he gave me his robe and his sword and his allegiance. How can I be a blessing to his surviving family today?"

And there was a servant of the house of Saul whose name was Ziba. So when they had called him to David, the king said to him, "Are you Ziba?" He said, "At your service!" Then the king said, "Is there not still someone of the house of Saul, to whom I may show the kindness of God?" And Ziba said to the king, "There is still a son of Jonathan who is lame in his feet."

So the king said to him, "Where is he?" And Ziba said to the king, "Indeed he is in the house of Machir the son of Ammiel, in Lo Debar." Then King David sent and brought him out of the house of Machir the son of Ammiel, from Lo Debar.

Now when Mephibosheth the son of Jonathan, the son of Saul, had come to David, he fell on his face and prostrated himself. Then David said, "Mephibosheth?" And he answered, "Here is your servant." So David said to him, "Do not fear, for I will surely show you kindness for Jonathan your father's sake and will restore to you all the land of Saul your grandfather; and you shall eat bread at my table continually." Then he bowed himself and said, "What is your servant that you should look upon such a dead dog as I?" — 2 Samuel 9:2-8

This story shows how when goodness is seeking to be a blessing, it is not tripped up by excuses or inconvenience. It's not looking for the easy way out. It does not expire or have a statute of limitation.

When David heard that a son of Jonathan was still alive, he thought he'd struck gold. David was fully committed to share God's goodness with Jonathan's son, but if he had been looking for a reason to back out, he would have found plenty of excuses. This man Mephibosheth was handicapped, which meant he'd be more difficult to take care of. It would be harder for

Mephibosheth to get around and besides, he wasn't even in Jerusalem. He was far away in a place called Lo Debar. In Hebrew, this means "no pasture" or "no communication." Translated into contemporary English, Lo Debar means "You can't get there from here. You can't even send a letter or make a phone call there. They never heard of cell phones in Lo Debar.'

In other words, Jonathan's son lived *nowhere*, in a place not even worth talking about. There were no pastures there. No animals. No food. No means of making a living. There's absolutely no reason to go there, unless a person intentionally wants to break away from all civilization. After King Saul was defeated in battle, Mephibosheth and his caretakers undoubtedly wanted to bunker down as far away as they could from the new administration. In fact, Mephibosheth was paralyzed at the age of five when his nurse dropped him as they were fleeing from the palace. He had not been able to walk ever since he was five.

So King David had absolutely every reason in the world to let sleeping dogs lie and say, "Well, at least I tried to do good for Jonathan and Saul's family."

But no! David didn't flinch when he heard that Jonathan's son was paralyzed and literally living in the middle of nowhere. He simply said, "Go get him."

When Mephibosheth eventually came before the king, he thought he was in trouble. Why else would King Saul's enemy, David, have hunted him down and brought him back from such a forsaken place? So David said, "Do not fear, for I will surely show you kindness for your father's sake."

Look at the extravagant goodness that sprang from David's heart. He said, "I will surely show you kindness for the sake of your father Jonathan. I will restore to you all the land that belonged to your grandfather Saul and you will always eat at my table."

When Mephibosheth heard that, he could hardly believe his ears. He bowed and said, "What is your servant that you should notice a dead dog like me?" That's the way he has seen himself since he was five years old. A dead dog. What good is a dead dog to anyone, let alone the king of Israel?

Here's how the chapter ends:

"As for Mephibosheth," said the king, "he shall eat at my table like one of the king's sons." Mephibosheth had a young son whose name was Micha. And all who dwelt in the house of Ziba were servants of Mephibosheth. So Mephibosheth dwelt in Jerusalem, for he ate continually at the king's table. And he was lame in both his feet. — 2 Samuel 9:11b-13

What an incredible testimony of God's goodness! One moment Mephibosheth is wiping the grit of no-man's land off his sweaty brow, and the next moment he's dining at the king's table. Isn't that a perfect picture of goodness! God's goodness will move you from Lo Debar to Jerusalem. It will take you from nothing and nowhere to Jerusalem, the City of Peace. That's what the name *Jerusalem* means: City of Peace. You may feel as if you've reached a dead end in life and maybe you have, but with God's goodness, you are one small step away from eating at the king's table in the City of Peace.

Don't miss the final words of chapter nine: "And he was lame in both feet."

See how God's goodness is not defined by our expectations. We might have expected some kind of Hollywood picture-perfect ending, with Mephibosheth receiving fame and fortune and physical healing. But there's a lesson here.

Sometimes God doesn't heal in the physical.

Sometimes He heals through goodness.

Sometimes He heals through undeserved blessings, through the kindness of people He has appointed to share His love. God blesses in many different ways and it's not always how we might expect.

However, one thing is certain. When God has blessed you, the best thing to do is to pay it forward. When He blesses, you can be certain He already has people in mind who need to be blessed by you. That's the beauty of the fruit of goodness. It increases by being given away. And it never diminishes, unless it remains buried in your heart.

"A good man out of the good treasure of his heart brings forth good things ..." — Matthew 12:35

Find someone who can't repay you and out of the treasure of your heart, share some good things with them. Do right by them, whether you think they deserve it or not. Find somebody living nowhere — somebody who has nothing worth talking about — and help them move to a place of peace. Help them move to a place of goodness.

Help them move to a place of provision. Feed them at your table. Give them a place to rest their head. And as you do that — seeking no reward for yourself — discover how the act of sharing goodness is the best reward you can ever hope for.

Abide in the Lord and you will bear much fruit!

Faithfulness

But the fruit of the
Spirit is love, joy, peace,
longsuffering, kindness,
*goodness, **faithfulness**,*
gentleness and self-control.
— Galatians 5:22-23

Galatians 5 tells us that the fruit of the Spirit is faithfulness. The obvious fact that shouldn't be missed is that you can't be faithful if you don't have some things to be faithful over. You need some responsibilities. The Lord gives us the fruit of faithfulness because He has entrusted some things to us. He wants us to be dependable toward people and situations, but thankfully He's not like the boss who tells us what to do but never shows us how to do it. Because God is faithful, He demonstrates His trustworthiness to us. He shows us how to be dependable to others.

Here's our definition of faithfulness: ***trustworthiness in relationships, responsibilities and resources.***

In describing this fruit of the Spirit, Paul uses the Greek word *pistis*, meaning "faithfulness." It's a common word in the New Testament — used about 240 times — although it is usually translated as "faith." Only three times is it translated as "faithfulness."[12] For example:

> *For by grace you have been saved through faith and that not of yourselves; it is the gift of God, not of works, lest anyone should boast.* — Ephesians 2:8-9

That word "faith" is translated from the Greek *pistis*. This is a helpful explanation of our salvation. The first few words make it clear that we are saved by grace, which is God's unmerited favor. It's an undeserved gift from God because of His love for us. Salvation comes from God by grace, but how does it get to us? That's where *pistis* comes in. Paul says that grace comes "through faith." In other words, faith is the vehicle that drove grace into your life. Faith is the Uber. Faith picked up the grace and drove it into your life. Uber wouldn't have anything to deliver if God hadn't provided that salvation by His grace. That salvation is a gift of God so nobody can boast. Even the Uber driver can't boast. God gets all the credit for that salvation, although we'll never possess it if we don't exercise *pistis*.

This passage illustrates the trustworthiness of God. He made a promise that we need to believe. We must put our trust in His promise. Salvation means putting trust in the trustworthiness of God. This is the essence of faith and faithfulness.

The Greek word *pistis* is used again in the following context:

---

[12] Matthew 23:23; Galatians 5:22; Philemon 1:5.

For we walk by faith, not by sight. — 2 Corinthians 5:7

Again, this illustrates our dependence on the trustworthiness of God. He made promises to us, contingent upon our walking in obedience and trust and integrity and truth, even when the world's advice is going contrary to God's advice. Faithfulness means basing every step we take and every decision we make on the trustworthiness of God.

Our entire lives are dependent upon God being trustworthy. Faith mandates that we depend on Him rather than on what we see. Jesus said that making decisions based on what we see and feel is like building a house on sinking sand (Matthew 7:24-27). Wise believers will live by faith, building on the solid rock of God's promises. His trustworthiness is the rock upon which we stand.

Each morning say, "Lord, I don't know how I'm going to get through this day but I trust you. You are faithful so I will be faithful too. I don't know how you will get me through some of these challenges but I trust you. You've brought me here and I believe you won't abandon me now. Your Spirit empowers me to overcome and to be more than a conqueror in Christ. I stand on your promises. Fulfill your word in my life today."

In scripture, *pistis* is usually translated as "faith." But in Galatians 5:22, the same word is translated as "faithfulness." Why? Because here the focus is not only on you and God, but on the fruit that faith bears in your relationships, responsibilities and resources. God is faithful to you. You are faithful to Him. The next step that embodies the fruit of the Spirit is for you to be faithful and dependable to others.

With that as a background, let's dig deeper into what faithfulness actually looks like.

Being Trustworthy in Relationships

God wants to make us trustworthy in three areas. First, He needs us to *be trustworthy in relationships*. This is the core of faithfulness and it is especially important in an age when faithfulness is very hard to find.

What does faithfulness look like?

To answer that question, we need to understand first and foremost that *God is faithful*. Many Bible passages talk about the faithfulness of God. For example, 1 Corinthians 10:13 simply says that "God is faithful." However, to obtain a deeper understanding of His character, we need to look at the context of that passage:

> *Therefore let him who thinks he stands take heed lest he fall. No temptation has overtaken you except such as is common to man; but God is faithful, who will not allow you to be tempted beyond what you are able, but with the temptation will also make the way of escape, that you may be able to bear it.* — 1 Corinthians 10:12-13

Think for a moment about the phrase that reads "let him who thinks he stands." Like the Corinthian church, we say:

I got this covered.
I'm good.
No problem here.

I don't need any help.

Paul is saying, "You think you're good but watch out. Take heed lest you fall." If you ever lived in a cold climate, you might have learned this the hard way. You came charging out the door without taking heed, not knowing there was a sheet of ice coating the driveway, and — *WHAM!!!* — in a flash, you're flat on your back. To avoid breaking everything you got, you need to come out looking like your granny, holding onto everything you possibly can.

That's the revelation here. If you think you stand, be careful. Why? Because not every fall is the product of weakness. It might be due to carelessness. It might be due to distractions. It's not always weakness so you have to be very careful lest you fall. You can't assume everything is okay. Take heed. Be careful lest you fall.

Paul says that no temptation is uncommon. No temptation is unique. You feel as if you're the only one to go through this temptation but you're not. It's common to everyone. In fact, the scripture warns about three major categories of sin: the lust of the flesh, the lust of the eyes and the pride of life (1 John 2:16). When Satan came to tempt Jesus in the wilderness, he gave Jesus each one of these types of temptations (Matthew 4:1-11). He dealt with the lust of the flesh, the lust of the eyes and the pride of life. It's helpful to recognize that all temptations fall into these categories and to know that you're not the only one experiencing them. The enemy knows how to drop a specific, customized temptation in your lap, personalized to your desires and weaknesses. He doesn't try to get you to fall in the areas of your greatest strength and preparedness.

Satan tempted Jesus with bread when He was at His point of greatest weakness, while He was fasting for 40 days in the desert. Satan specializes in customized temptation. He knows your preferences. He's been studying you. The temptation might seem unique and custom fit to your preferences, but in fact it's the same old temptation that other folk have been experiencing over and over again.

You know it's a temptation custom fit for you if it grabs you like a magnet. If that person hitting on you at the gym doesn't turn you on, it's not a serious temptation from Satan. But you know they're hand-picked by the enemy when you're forced to cry out, "Oh, help me Jesus! I need you right now!" The devil knows how to ring your bell so take heed lest you fall.

After Paul tells us that no temptation is uncommon, he says, "but God is faithful." Here's the good news. God is faithful! He will always set us up to succeed. Then Paul assures us that God won't let any temptations go beyond what we are able to bear. In fact, He will give us a means of escape so we will be able to deal with it. He set us up to win! He built in a way of escape! Why? Because He is faithful.

So the first thing to know about faithfulness is that *God is faithful*.

Second, since God is faithful to us, we must be *faithful to Him*. Jesus said:

"If you love me, keep my commandments. And I will pray the Father and He will give you another Helper, that He may abide with you forever ..." — John 14:15-16

You prove your love with actions, not words. God says, "Don't say you love me if you regularly live in disobedience to me. Don't say you honor me while ignoring my will for your life. If you love me, show me the evidence by keeping my commandments."

This is true in all human relationships. If you say you love someone, that love is proven by the evidence. If somebody says they love you but doesn't do anything to back their words up, it's time to send them away. There's no place for fake love in our relationships.

However, don't beat yourself up if you make a mistake and want to do better. Anybody can have a bad day. Authentic love demands that we come back and say, "I shouldn't have spoken to you like that. I shouldn't have acted like that. I'm sorry. Will you please forgive me?" The two golden words of love are *I'm sorry.*

Some people look like their lips weren't built to say certain words. They try to say "I was wrong," and it's like jamming a square peg in a round hole. If someone doesn't know how to say "I'm sorry," know that you will never have more than a superficial relationship with them. You can't trust that kind of fake love.

True love doubles back. It says, "Please forgive me." It tries to undo the damage. And next time, it learns from its mistakes and tries to do better.

When Jesus told us to keep His commandments, He knew we were human. He knew we would fail sometimes. So He said, "Here's what I'm going to do. I'll give you a Helper." That's the Holy Spirit, the third person of the Trinity. When the Holy Spirit came to the early church, He brought all the power and wisdom and strength of the Godhead with Him. This Helper knows you have certain weaknesses so He gives you wisdom and strength to be victorious.

What an amazing plan! It's wonderful to know that while the Holy Spirit abides in us, it's okay to say, "I can't do it. I'm not strong enough. I'm too weak." That's okay because the Holy Spirit comes in and brings strength. And in fact, nobody is strong enough to overcome sin on their own, so you might as well acknowledge your weakness and go straight to the Helper. God knows you are weak. That's why He sent the Holy Spirit. He is setting you up to succeed. He wants you to live the victorious life.

So, the first thing to know about faithfulness is that *God is faithful to us*.

Second, He calls us to be *faithful to Him*.

Third, God calls us to be *faithful in our relationships with others*. That means we need to know how to cultivate dependable relationships.

Three Examples of Dependable Relationships

Let me give you three examples of dependable

relationships. First, *God calls us to be dependable in marriage*. He calls spouses to be faithful to each other. The Bible says:

> ... *let each man have his own wife and let each woman have her own husband. Let the husband render to his wife the affection due her and likewise also the wife to her husband.* — 1 Corinthians 7:2-3

God wants you to be a dependable husband or wife. He knows that you have some weaknesses and that's why He sent you the Helper. You're not alone. He's right beside you, helping you to live this out. When you fall short, repent and say those golden words and mean them. Say "I'm sorry." Then let the Holy Spirit teach you how to be what God wants you to be in this relationship.

The Bible is very practical. It doesn't say, "Let each man have two or three ..." It tells us exactly what a healthy marriage looks like. Give that special wife or husband all the affection they deserve. And whether you want to confess it or not, God is pleased to bless these relationships with sexual intimacy. Some folk act like God frowns at sex or that He pretends it doesn't happen. The fact is He created it! The fact is He blesses the marriage bed in a special way.

So first, we're called to be *dependable in marriage*.

Secondly, we're called to be *dependable in friendships*. King Solomon wrote:

> *A friend loves at all times and a brother is born for adversity.* — Proverbs 17:17

In our world, it's easier to get a fan than a friend. Fans love you because of what they can get out of you. They love you because of your reputation. You do something clever or funny and they give you a "Like." That's not a true friend.

A true friend is born for adversity. They love you at all times, but that love is felt most in the difficult moments. They are not the kind of smiley faces you only see on sunny days. Fair-weather friends are the last things you need! You are more than capable of enjoying a beautiful day all by yourself. But when all hell is breaking loose ... that's when you really need a friend. When King Saul was trying to catch and kill David, Jonathan pledged his life to David, to help and defend him. That's the kind of friend you need.

You need people who will mourn with you when you mourn. You also need people who will rejoice with you when you rejoice. You don't need the kind of friend who is jealous or holds a grudge when you succeed in an area where they can't. When you are celebrating your greatest victory or achievement, you need friends who show up with cake and prizes and party favors. A true friend is born for adversity, but a true friend also knows how to party! A true friend is not going to roll their eyes because you got engaged or promoted and they didn't.

When you've made a bad mess of things, you need somebody who loves you enough to help you deal with it. You also need a friend who will say, "Hey. Can I see you for a minute? Can we talk?" When you hear that, you know they have something important that needs to be addressed. You ask yourself, "Did I say or do something inappropriate?"

Solomon also wrote:

Faithful are the wounds of a friend but the kisses of an enemy are deceitful. — Proverbs 27:6

We saw this principle in action in the section on *phileo* love. When a friend cuts, they cut to heal, like a doctor. When an enemy cuts, they cut to bring you down. One cuts to kill. The other cuts to heal. Know that a true friend loves you enough to walk with you through even the painful parts of healing.

God calls us to be *dependable in marriage.*
He calls us to be *dependable in friendship.*
Finally, God calls us to be *dependable in ministry.*

A wonderful case study of dependable ministry comes from the relationship between Barnabas and John Mark, which we studied in the chapter on Goodness. To review, we learned that Paul and Barnabas were accompanied in their first missionary trip by John Mark, whose mother led one of the house churches in Jerusalem. John Mark was used to being in a nice and cozy Christian atmosphere, which explains why he went AWOL when they encountered hostility in their ministry. He abandoned Paul and Barnabas and went back home.

Later in Acts 15, Paul and Barnabas decided to go on a second mission trip. But when Barnabas suggested bringing

John Mark, Paul said, "No way. He bailed out on us once. He got homesick and went home to his mama. I'm not bringing him again."

Barnabas said, "Come on, Paul. Give him a chance to learn from his mistakes. He's got a good heart."

But Paul wouldn't have it. Eventually their disagreement was so strong that they split, with Paul choosing Silas as his companion and Barnabas choosing John Mark.

You can hardly blame them for disagreeing. Paul had a good point but so did Barnabas. Paul's strong temperament made it difficult for him to see another point of view. Nobody could say Paul was being unreasonable or un-Christian. He was just being practical. As for Barnabas, scripture calls him the "son of encouragement" (Acts 4:36). His temperament drove him to give John Mark another chance and train him as they traveled, so that's exactly what happened. Later in the story we see how John Mark had matured significantly and how he had become a dependable part of the team.

One lesson here is to not throw people away just because they make a mistake. You might need to distance yourself from them until they get some things together, but don't cut them off permanently. Maybe God brought them into your life for a purpose. Maybe you need to squash your pride and stop going through the list of reasons why you should dismiss them. God might be appointing you to disciple them to a place of maturity. And if you have trouble humbling yourself, ask God to jog your memory about the times where you could have and should have been thrown away, but someone had the grace and mercy to put an arm around you and bring you to a better place.

In fact, each one of us has been the recipient of more grace than we realize. And how dare we, the recipients of God's abundant blessings, turn around and start throwing people out so quickly? It's like when God was bringing non-Jews into the church for the first time. At that time, folk like Peter really struggled with that concept. They had been steeped in a long tradition of Jews being special, so their natural tendency was to send all the Gentiles away. That's when God gave Peter a vision in which he was told to eat the unclean animals that Jews were forbidden from eating (Acts 10). Meanwhile, God spoke to a Gentile named Cornelius, who invited Peter to come speak at his house. Peter accepted the invitation, even though he'd never walked in the door of a Gentile before. The most amazing part of the story is how when Peter started preaching, the Holy Ghost fell on the Gentiles just like He'd fallen on the Jewish Christians at Pentecost.

While Peter was still speaking these words, the Holy Spirit came on all who heard the message. The circumcised believers who had come with Peter were astonished that the gift of the Holy Spirit had been poured out even on Gentiles. For they heard them speaking in tongues and praising God. Then Peter said, "Surely no one can stand in the way of their being baptized with water. They have received the Holy Spirit just as we have." So he ordered that they be baptized in the name of Jesus Christ. Then they asked Peter to stay with them for a few days. — Acts 10:44-47 (NIV)

This story is just as relevant today as it was in the first century. God is calling His people to open their hearts. Don't cut off the people God wants to minister to. His faithfulness demands that we be faithful too. He needs us to be dependable.

In summary, God calls us to be trustworthy in three areas of relationships: in marriage, in friendships and in ministry.

Being Trustworthy in Responsibilities

In the previous section, we saw how God calls us to be trustworthy in our relationships. He also calls us to be trustworthy in responsibilities.

Jesus said:

"Whoever can be trusted with very little can also be trusted with much, and whoever is dishonest with very little will also be dishonest with much." — Luke 16:10 (NIV)

If you want to be dependable in major, future responsibilities, learn to handle the little things first. How dependable are you with responsibilities that seem less important or more mundane? Don't wait to develop trustworthiness later, because your days are numbered. You might live to be 80 or 90, or you might only have until next week. Don't take life for granted. Maximize your opportunities today.

Being dependable means doing the right thing today, no matter how small or mundane your calling might seem to be. Your time is finite so don't waste it. Down time is not wasted time. You need to chill out at times to recharge your reserves. That's why God gave us the Sabbath, so we can rest and recharge. Then when you're working, manage your talents properly.

Jesus taught us how to be trustworthy with our responsibilities in the Parable of the Talents. Jesus said:

> *"For the kingdom of heaven is like a man traveling to a far country who called his own servants and delivered his goods to them. And to one he gave five talents, to another two and to another one, to each according to his own ability; and immediately he went on a journey. Then he who had received the five talents went and traded with them and made another five talents. And likewise he who had received two gained two more also. But he who had received one went and dug in the ground and hid his lord's money. After a long time the lord of those servants came and settled accounts with them.*
>
> *"So he who had received five talents came and brought five other talents, saying, 'Lord, you delivered to me five talents; look, I have gained five more talents besides them.' His lord said to him, 'Well done, good and faithful servant; you were faithful over a few things, I will make you ruler over many things. Enter into the joy of your lord.' He also who had received two talents came and said, 'Lord, you delivered to me two talents; look, I have gained two more talents besides them.' His lord said to him, 'Well done, good and faithful servant; you have been faithful over a few things, I will make you ruler over many things. Enter into the joy of your lord.'*

"Then he who had received the one talent came and said, 'Lord, I knew you to be a hard man, reaping where you have not sown and gathering where you have not scattered seed. And I was afraid and went and hid your talent in the ground. Look, there you have what is yours.'

"But his lord answered and said to him, 'You wicked and lazy servant, you knew that I reap where I have not sown and gather where I have not scattered seed. So you ought to have deposited my money with the bankers and at my coming I would have received back my own with interest. So take the talent from him and give it to him who has ten talents. For to everyone who has, more will be given and he will have abundance; but from him who does not have, even what he has will be taken away.'" — Matthew 25:14-29

We see how this master called his servants to account after returning from his journey. The first two servants gave him a 100 percent return on his investment, so they were blessed generously in return. "Well done, good and faithful servant," they were told. Unfortunately, the third servant buried his talent, which meant he ended up with no reward in the end.

God's gifts and callings are to be used for His kingdom, not to be sat upon. We have to use them or lose them. Don't be like that lazy servant who, when the master returned, said, "Well, ah … see what happened wuz …" You may have good "intentions" of using your gifts to help others someday, but this story warns you not to delay. We don't know when the master is returning. And when He does, He expects a return on the gifts and talents He's given you. Don't expect abundant blessings to multiply around you when you are sitting on the gifts and talents that God has given you.

Be like Joseph, one of the twelve sons of Jacob. He had been betrayed by his brothers and sold into slavery in Egypt, where he found himself working as a servant in the house of an influential man named Potiphar. Genesis 39 tells how dependable Joseph was. He found favor in Potiphar's household and was promoted to be the domestic manager. The Lord blessed Him for his faithfulness. God even blessed Potiphar's household for Joseph's sake.

> *From the time he put him in charge of his household and of all that he owned, the Lord blessed the household of the Egyptian because of Joseph. The blessing of the Lord was on everything Potiphar had, both in the house and in the field. So Potiphar left everything he had in Joseph's care; with Joseph in charge, he did not concern himself with anything except the food he ate.* — Genesis 39:5-6 (NIV)

That's what God will do through you, but He needs you to be dependable. Your employer will be blessed because of your faithfulness. Don't believe you aren't having a positive impact on your coworkers just because they don't know the Lord. See how God blessed Potiphar's entire household because of Joseph. Potiphar didn't have to worry about a thing! His only concern was the food he ate.

Be like Joseph. Give your employer nothing to be concerned about. Be faithful in the little things. When your coworkers are concerned about that nagging assignment, do all you can to be able to say, "I got it covered. No problem.

No worries."

Faithfulness means being trustworthy in your responsibilities. Get a solid reputation for being dependable. That's the practical nature of the fruit of the Spirit. Faithfulness is not all about being holy and religious-sounding. It means getting your hands dirty and earning a reputation for being dependable.

Being Trustworthy in Resources

We have seen how faithfulness means, first, being *trustworthy in our relationships*.

Second, faithfulness is being *trustworthy in our responsibilities*.

Third, faithfulness means being *trustworthy in our resources*.

How trustworthy are you with your resources? Even if you think you don't have much, how faithful are you with what you have? Are you faithful in the little things?

I can't tell you how many times I've heard someone say, "Pastor, I have some big things about to break. My ship is coming in. Oh Pastor, when this hits, it's going to be big. When I get this sum of money, I'm going to start giving big-time to the kingdom of God!" I had one person say their windfall would be so enormous that they were on the verge of tithing a million dollars. The problem is, this promise wasn't consistent with their record of giving only twos and fews. How could someone expect to give a million when they couldn't be faithful in the little things? Jesus was right. You need to be trustworthy with what you have now if you ever expect to do big things in the future.

When we moved to California in 1989, I began working for a church with 34 members. The budget for the entire year was $60,000. Out of that, they said they could pay me $24,000. Simple math tells you that our growing family had just $2,000 a month to live on. The first thing we did with that salary was to set aside $200 each month for the Lord. That left us with just $1,800 to cover all our family needs. That sum would have worked out well back in the hood in Philadelphia, where there was a crack house across the street and a monthly mortgage of $200. But in California, when I told folk I was praying for a house to rent for under $1,000 a month, they thought I ought to go see a psychiatrist. But we knew that if God had called us to California, He would make it possible for us to live there.

And He did. Someone in the property management office made a divine mistake by writing $995 on our rental paperwork. When I went to sign it, the lady said, "This place shouldn't have rented for less than $1,250. Someone wrote $995 by mistake." But she let me sign it anyway. After that, God provided for every financial need we had out of that slim monthly salary. We had just enough to buy food, clothes, insurance and gas for the car. God was faithful in meeting our needs month after month. But the first thing we did was to set aside a tithe for the Lord.

If you can't give God a tithe out of your low income, don't hope to do big things when your ship comes in. Some people say, "I can't afford to be generous. I don't have much." That's not true. In God's economy, you can't afford *not* to be generous. Like we saw in the Parable of the Talents, never expect abundant blessings and prosperity when you are sitting on the gifts that God has given you.

Here are four practical points for maximizing your giving, and they all start with the letter S:

1) Sow generously. Tithing is simple. When you receive a sum of money, just shift the decimal point over one space to the left and that's your tithe. Give more if you can. Don't think for a minute that 90 percent is yours, because the whole thing belongs to God's. When Jesus said, "Seek first the kingdom of God," that includes giving first and foremost to God. Start with ten percent. As your joy and generosity increase, consider giving more. You may discover that you need less than you thought you did to live on. Sow generously and you will reap generous benefits in God's kingdom.

2) Shrink debt systematically. God didn't put you in debt. You put you in debt. Now it's time to shrink that debt. There are several financial programs developed by Christian leaders that teach good debt management. Use them to knock out debt. Then shift that money toward your savings.

3) Save regularly. Don't say you can't afford to save, because you can start with quarters in a jar if that's all you have. Set aside a dollar a day, then bump it up to two, bump two up to four, four up to ten and keep going. When an emergency comes someday, you can never say you didn't see it coming ... because it will come! You know it will come, so save now. If you're living hand to mouth, you will have no margin for a broken-down car or medical emergency, so put something away now. Not everything

you make today is for today. Even the ants know how to store up food for the lean times that are coming (Proverbs 6). So trust that God will meet your needs. Even if times are tight, make a regular practice of saving.

4) Spend wisely. If you are not in a good financial place, stop acting like you are. That means learning to delay gratification. You can't always buy what you want. Stop going out to eat. Be trustworthy with your finances by asking the Lord to help you delay gratification when your desire for something is strong. Learn to say, "No, I won't buy this. I might want it right now but I can't afford it right now. I'm learning to spend wisely." Don't buy designer clothes if this is your K-Mart season. The Holy Spirit is more than qualified to walk in and show you what to wear. He is changing your patterns and teaching you to say "No."

Learn to be trustworthy in your relationships, your responsibilities and your resources. This is what faithfulness looks like — being trustworthy and dependable in all these areas. Get a reputation for bearing the fruit of faithfulness and you will bring much glory to God.

Abide in the Lord and you will bear much fruit!

Gentleness

But the fruit of the
Spirit is love, joy, peace,
longsuffering, kindness,
goodness, faithfulness,
gentleness *and self-control.*
— Galatians 5:22-23

We have covered seven of the fruit mentioned in Galatians 5:23, the gifts that God has given us for fruitful living. As we unpack this eighth fruit, gentleness, you might be surprised. It's much deeper and richer than you might expect. It's not being quiet and easygoing and meek. As we study God's word together, I pray that your understanding of the need for the fruit of gentleness will grow deeper and richer.

How might we describe gentleness? ***Gentleness is strength under control.***

Some Bibles have translated this word as "meekness," which is misleading in modern English. A more accurate rendering is *strength under control*. Be assured that meekness is not weakness. Some people think that a gentle person is a wimp. To be meek is not to be weak. Jesus never said, "Blessed are the weak." He never taught His

209

followers to be wimps. On the contrary, their strength and control led them to stand in gentle confidence in the face of tremendous opposition and persecution. They were anything but wimps.

God doesn't make wimps. Too many passive Christians mistakenly believe that God sanctions their weakness when in fact, they themselves are responsible for being disempowered. God never said it's okay to let people trample you and take advantage of you. If you are overly passive, that's your own choice, not God's. Even if you are naturally weak, you can develop godly *strength under control* as you cultivate the fruit of gentleness in your life.

An Entirely New Picture of Gentleness

To deepen your understanding of gentleness, begin by painting a mental picture of a physically powerful man in your head. This man has a chiseled body with a well-defined six-pack. His biceps are bulging and his thighs are like tree trunks. This dude is straight-up cut. Now some of you sisters are probably shifting in your seats saying, "Whew, praise God! The fruit of the Spirit never looked so good!" That's fine. I just want you to get this man in your mind.

Now picture this same man holding a tiny infant in his hands. He's cuddling this infant, holding it close, smiling, looking straight into its eyes. Picture him gently rocking that child, humming a little tune in the child's ear. You can see a pleasant smile on that baby's face. After a while, the child's eyes start to droop. The man keeps rocking and humming and adoring his precious little baby until, before long, the child is fast asleep. So he very carefully sets the baby in a crib for its nap.

Later, imagine the child stirring, so that strong, chiseled man picks the baby up and holds it close. Both are smiling now, as he coos and kisses and tickles the baby. You can see the child giggle and laugh and smile at its daddy. Soon the man changes the baby's diaper and places it in a little swing in the living room where it's safe and comfortable. Then he pops into the kitchen to make up a bottle for the baby and grab a snack for himself.

He's only gone for a few minutes when he hears the child crying. So he returns to the living room, where he is shocked to see that a stranger has climbed in through a window, grabbed the baby and is intent upon escaping with the child. As you can imagine, the father's gentle face and strong demeanor instantly changes. He transforms. In that man you can see the same strength, but it manifests itself in a very different way. That chiseled man now uses his brute, physical strength to subdue the intruder and rescue his child. If necessary, he is prepared to disassemble that man piece by piece with his bare hands to get his baby back.

Anything could happen here, but if he is walking in the fruit of the Spirit and especially the fruit of gentleness, he will incapacitate the intruder only enough to hold him down long enough to get him into the hands of the authorities. The fruit of gentleness will lead him to subdue the guy for the sake of the child, while not acting out of anger or hatred or vengeance. He might be able to justify killing the guy, but *strength under control* tells him that's not necessary. He would only be killing the man out of spite. So he uses his gentle strength to knock the guy unconscious, get the baby to safety and call 9-1-1. He knows that if he does anything rash, he might go to jail and that would jeopardize the child's future. He needs to be present to raise that child. So in gentleness, he uses his strength only within the proper boundaries.

This is a picture of gentleness. This is strength under control. For the fruit of gentleness to be present, you need both strength and control. Strength without control lacks the fruit of gentleness. So does wimpiness. Weakness lacks gentleness. An unassertive person will be paralyzed in life, unable to pursue the destiny that God has ordained. Such a person will be desperately in need of the fruit of gentleness. True gentleness will bring strength in the Lord with godly control.

That's what Paul meant when he said, "The fruit of the Spirit is gentleness."

Strong and Gentle Jesus

If you want to discover the best picture of gentleness, look to Jesus. He came to model each fruit of the Spirit for us, including gentleness. That fact was described by Luke, who said this about the early years of Jesus:

And Jesus increased in wisdom and stature and in favor with God and men. — Luke 2:52

Here we see how Jesus increased in four areas: in wisdom, in stature, in favor with God and in favor with man. Although Jesus was fully God, He was also born fully human. During these developmental years, He became physically, spiritually, socially and emotionally mature. At the age of 30, Jesus went to be baptized by His cousin John (Matthew 3:13-17), showing us that we need to be baptized too. Everything He did was an example for us. He showed us how to cultivate each fruit of the Spirit.

That's why it's so important to study the fruit of gentleness in the life of Jesus. Jesus was a paradox. On the one hand, He is the strongest person who ever lived. He is strength personified. He's not a fantasy, like Greek myths or Hollywood superheroes. He's in a completely different class than Marvel Comic heroes. Jesus is simply the strongest man you will ever know. He said:

> *"All authority has been given to me in heaven and on earth."* — Matthew 28:18b

If Jesus had wanted to, He could have exercised more power than Caesar and Napoleon and every modern superpower combined. He had all the power and authority in the world. But He was much more than an earthly ruler. He was much more than a king.

Jesus is the *"King of kings and Lord of lords"* (1 Timothy 6:15; Revelations 17:14; Revelations 19:16). He is the *"ruler of the kings of the earth"* (Revelations 1:5). Every president and king and ruler will bow before Jesus and acknowledge that He is Lord. Every governor and congressman and senator will bow. Even Hitler and Stalin will bow before Him. The common folk like you and I will also bow before Him. The Bible says:

*Therefore God also has highly exalted Him and given
Him the name which is above every name, that at the
name of Jesus every knee should bow, of those in
heaven and of those on earth and of those under the
earth and that every tongue should confess that Jesus
Christ is Lord, to the glory of God the Father.* —
Philippians 2:9-11

Every knee will bow. Every tongue will confess. If you
are reluctant to surrender your life to Jesus, why not do it
now? Better to bow sooner than later, so you can enjoy His
grace in this life and the next. He is the strongest man who
ever lived but He doesn't push His power around. With
open arms, He invites you to be a joint-heir with Him in
His kingdom. If you haven't done so already, ask Him to
forgive your sins and transform your life. Then get yourself
into a loving Christian fellowship; a Bible-teaching church.
God loves you more than you can imagine and He wants to
welcome you into His family. So why not bow before Him
today?

Praise God for showing us His amazing character in the
life of Jesus Christ. While Jesus was undoubtedly the
strongest man who ever lived, He is also the gentlest. In the
Gospel of Matthew, Jesus said:

*"Come to me all you who labor and are heavy-laden
and I will give you rest. Take my yoke upon you and
learn from me, for I am gentle and lowly in heart and
you will find rest for your souls."* — Matthew 11:28-29

"For I am gentle," says Jesus. That's the same Greek
root as in Galatians 5:23. So Jesus, the greatest and most
powerful man who ever lived, said, "Come here and let me

show you about my character. Walk with me and learn from me. Of course, I'm powerful, but I don't flaunt that. I don't need to. I have this quiet strength that lets everyone know I'm not a wimp. Learn from my gentleness. Come alongside me and you will find rest for your soul."

Jesus was strength personified, but his strength was constantly under control. Jesus got lit and blasted people. His gentleness showed us how to exercise strength under control. We constantly see signs of Jesus' strength in His earthly ministry, in the way He ministered to people through teaching, healing, restoring the fallen, forgiving sinners and bringing hope to the disenfranchised. Strength guided His mission and kept Him from wavering. The Gospels are filled with examples of Jesus exercising gentleness and patience with people who were pushy and demanding.

In John's Gospel, we read about a time when Jesus intentionally restrained Himself, not allowing His power to go too far:

Now the Passover of the Jews was at hand and Jesus went up to Jerusalem. And He found in the temple those who sold oxen and sheep and doves and the money changers doing business. When He had made a whip of cords, He drove them all out of the temple, with the sheep and the oxen, and poured out the changers' money and overturned the tables. And He said to those who sold doves, "Take these things away! Do not make my Father's house a house of merchandise!" — John 2:13-16

When Jesus saw all this merchandising and profiteering

in a place of godly worship and devotion, He went off. But meanwhile, He restrained Himself and used His power to take people to a place where they could reevaluate their actions and hopefully make some positive changes.

We read in verse 15 how "He made a whip of cords." That's how far He was willing to go to clear the temple of evil men who were extorting temple-goers. They were selling sacrificial animals to out-of-town visitors who didn't have any choice but to pay their unfair prices. Jesus wasn't politely saying, "If it's not too difficult, I'd like you all to move out of here when you find it convenient." No! He drove them out with a whip. He cleared the temple area of this abomination. He despised how they were profaning the temple of God and He refused to put on a front. He let His righteous indignation be evident in action. He exemplified strength under control.

Jesus knew exactly where to restrain Himself. He exercised strength while not going too far. There's nothing wimpy about Jesus tossing tables and whipping people. He was getting it done, but without malice or permanent injury. He was showing His followers what not to tolerate and how to make demands while exercising control.

Another excellent example comes from the Gospel of Matthew. Here Jesus was speaking to His disciples in the Garden of Gethsemane on the night of His betrayal:

While He was still speaking, Judas, one of the Twelve, arrived. With him was a large crowd armed with swords and clubs, sent from the chief priests and the elders of the people. Now the betrayer had arranged a signal with them: "The one I kiss is the man; arrest Him." Going at once to Jesus, Judas said, "Greetings, Rabbi!" and kissed Him.

Jesus replied, "Do what you came for, friend." Then the men stepped forward, seized Jesus and arrested Him. With that, one of Jesus' companions reached for his sword, drew it out and struck the servant of the high priest, cutting off his ear. "Put your sword back in its place," Jesus said to him, "for all who draw the sword will die by the sword. Do you think I cannot call on my Father and He will at once put at my disposal more than twelve legions of angels? But how then would the scriptures be fulfilled that say it must happen in this way?" — Matthew 26:47-54 (NIV)

When one of Jesus' followers drew his sword, he wasn't aiming for the servant's ear. That's not why folk swing swords at people. Without question, he was trying to shorten the man by a head, but he barely missed, cutting off an ear.

Jesus said, "Put that thing away. I don't need you defending me like that. I'm powerful enough. I have authority enough. I could call this off right now if I wanted to. I could have legions of angels here at the snap of my fingers. But that's not the path I've chosen. I need to go through some hard things for the good of all mankind so the scriptures will be fulfilled."

This is a perfect picture of strength under control. He was gentle of spirit in the face of the most cruel, deceptive betrayal by a close friend who in the act, kissed Him and called Him "friend." Nobody on earth could display that kind of strength under control without the fully-cultivated fruit of gentleness in their life. That's what Jesus was showing us.

If you ever had someone you love turn against you and cause you all manner of harm, you will begin to understand how Jesus felt. Maybe someone you love stole from you, cheated on you or spread false rumors about you. That kind of pain of betrayal can lead you to use all the strength at your disposal to destroy them once and for all. And yet Jesus, whose betrayal led to a brutal death on the cross, displayed such a beautiful strength under control. He said, "Now is not the time to fight back. Step down your display of power. In time, even these knees will bow to me. But not now. Be gentle, even in the face of this betrayal."

There is a time to do exactly that — to step down and respond with quietness. There is also a time to go off like Jesus did in the temple, but both responses require strength under control. You need the fruit of gentleness so you won't go overboard and catch a criminal case. The fruit of gentleness will allow you to put negative emotions like hatred and anger in their places. And when you abide in Christ — clinging to the vine and cultivating every fruit of the Spirit in harmony — the Holy Spirit will give you the wisdom to know when it's appropriate to stand and speak for God's truth and when it's time keep quiet and wait for the right time to act.

Jesus had the potential to go off and hurt some people but He chose, instead, to keep it under control and not go too far. In the same way, He wants to give you that power in your life today.

Gentleness in the Life of David

The Bible has many examples of godly men and women who acted with the gentle spirit of strength under control. The life of David presents us with an excellent case study.

After David brought down Goliath and began to lead military campaigns, his popularity with the Jews increased so much that he actually attracted a group of cheerleaders. He'd return from battle and the women would dance in the streets, singing, "Saul has slain his thousands and David his tens of thousands." Now when King Saul heard this — and how in the people's eyes, he was playing second fiddle to David — he developed a jealous spirit toward David. He said, "I'm not going to let this young buck take my glory." So he actively sought to kill David.

To save his life, David fled with his men into the wilderness where they lived like fugitives in caves.

Now it happened, when Saul had returned from following the Philistines, that it was told him, saying, "Take note! David is in the Wilderness of En Gedi." Then Saul took three thousand chosen men from all Israel and went to seek David and his men on the Rocks of the Wild Goats. So he came to the sheepfolds by the road, where there was a cave; and Saul went in to attend to his needs. (David and his men were staying in the recesses of the cave.) Then the men of David said to him, "This is the day of which the Lord said to you, 'Behold, I will deliver your enemy into your hand, that you may do to him as it seems good to you.' "

And David arose and secretly cut off a corner of Saul's robe. Now it happened afterward that David's heart troubled him because he had cut Saul's robe. And he said to his men, "The Lord forbid that I should do this thing to my master, the Lord's anointed, to stretch out my hand against him, seeing he is the anointed of the Lord." So David restrained his servants with these words and did not allow them to rise against Saul. And Saul got up from the cave and went on his way. David also arose afterward, went out of the cave and called out to Saul, saying, "My lord the king!" And when Saul looked behind him, David stooped with his face to the earth and bowed down.

And David said to Saul: "Why do you listen to the words of men who say, 'Indeed David seeks your harm'? Look, this day your eyes have seen that the Lord delivered you today into my hand in the cave and someone urged me to kill you. But my eye spared you and I said, 'I will not stretch out my hand against my lord, for he is the Lord's anointed.' Moreover, my father, see! Yes, see the corner of your robe in my hand! For in that I cut off the corner of your robe and did not kill you, know and see that there is neither evil nor rebellion in my hand and I have not sinned against you. Yet you hunt my life to take it. Let the Lord judge between you and me and let the Lord avenge me on you. But my hand shall not be against you. As the proverb of the ancients says, 'Wickedness proceeds from the wicked.' But my hand shall not be against you. After whom has the king of Israel come out? Whom do you pursue? A dead dog? A flea? Therefore let the Lord be judge and judge between you and me and see and plead my case and deliver me out of your hand."

So it was, when David had finished speaking these words to Saul, that Saul said, "Is this your voice, my son David?" And Saul lifted up his voice and wept. Then he said to David: "You are more righteous than I; for you have rewarded me with good, whereas I have rewarded you with evil. And you have shown this day how you have dealt well with me; for when the Lord delivered me into your hand, you did not kill me. For if a man finds his enemy, will he let him get away safely? Therefore may the Lord reward you with good for what you have done to me this day. And now I know indeed that you shall surely be king and that the kingdom of Israel shall be established in your hand. Therefore swear now to me by the Lord that you will not cut off my descendants after me and that you will not destroy my name from my father's house."

So David swore to Saul. And Saul went home, but David and his men went up to the stronghold. — 1 Samuel 24:1-22

In this story, we see David operating with amazing strength under control. Saul went into the same cave they were hiding in to go to the bathroom, but it's likely he also told his men, "That sun outside is wearing me out. It's nice and cool in here. I'm just going to shut my eyes for a few minutes."

When that happened, David's men said, "This is too good to be true! God has delivered this murderous king into your hands. Take him out! Now!"

But David wouldn't have it. Secretly, he cut off a corner of Saul's robe.

Wait a minute!

Cut off a corner of his robe?

What man in his right mind — in David's position — would not hesitate to cut that bad man's throat? He had every justification in the world. God had delivered his enemy into his hands.

And yet David cut off a corner of his robe. Now look at what he told his men:

"The Lord forbid that I should do such a thing to my master, the Lord's anointed, or lay my hand on him; for he is the anointed of the Lord."

David is on the run, hunted to the death by this blood-thirsty man, and yet he reminds his men of the time, long ago, when the Prophet Samuel anointed Saul to be king of Israel. David knew that Saul was still the Lord's anointed, even though he had lost all sense of godliness and sanity. David still respected that calling.

Just because someone is anointed by God doesn't mean God approves of everything they do. Let's be honest. Some anointed people have jacked-uptedness in their lives. Nobody is perfect, not even you. Not even me. We may be saved, sanctified and filled with the Holy Ghost, but our human nature is still jacked up in places. We're not perfect.

So David said, "This guy is the Lord's anointed. I won't harm him and you all don't harm him either." I love how when Saul left the cave, David got his attention from the hillside above. He called to Saul saying, "My lord the king." But David didn't stop there. He got down and pressed his face to the ground. He had the opportunity to take Saul out, once and for all, and yet he chose gentleness. He chose strength under control. In strength, he pledged not to harm Saul but to let the Lord be the judge between the two of them.

Notice how Saul wept and called David "my son." He was showing all the signs of repentance, but as you follow the story through, it's not long before Saul is back to hunting David again. It goes to show you that not everybody who's crying is truly remorseful about the things they have done. You can thank people for their tears and their words of apology, but if they aren't trustworthy, don't be fooled. They can still cause you harm and do you wrong. What's more, David didn't sugarcoat his language and pretend that everything was fine. In his gentleness, David asked the Lord to avenge the wrongs that Saul had done to him. Meanwhile, he understood his boundaries and refused to do the avenging himself. Here David shows us how to operate with strength under control, not with weakness and foolish behavior.

In this section of scripture, Saul confessed that God had, indeed, chosen David to be the next king of Israel. Then when Saul asked that his descendants not be cut off from his legacy, he displayed his self-centeredness. Even though Saul's faults were glaring, David still promised not to harm Saul's descendants. That plays out later, as we saw in the Faithfulness chapter, in how David wanted to bless Saul's grandson, Mephibosheth. David honored Mephibosheth by giving him a place of honor in Jerusalem and allowing him to eat at the king's table.

Two chapters later — in 1 Samuel 26 — Saul resumed his hunt for David in the Desert of Ziph with 3000 of his best soldiers.

So David arose and came to the place where Saul had encamped. And David saw the place where Saul lay and Abner the son of Ner, the commander of his army. Now Saul lay within the camp, with the people encamped all around him. Then David answered and said to Ahimelech the Hittite and to Abishai the son of Zeruiah, brother of Joab, saying, "Who will go down with me to Saul in the camp?" And Abishai said, "I will go down with you."

So David and Abishai came to the people by night; and there Saul lay sleeping within the camp, with his spear stuck in the ground by his head. And Abner and the people lay all around him. Then Abishai said to David, "God has delivered your enemy into your hand this day. Now therefore, please, let me strike him at once with the spear, right to the earth; and I will not have to strike him a second time!" But David said to Abishai, "Do not destroy him; for who can stretch out his hand against the Lord's anointed and be guiltless?" David said furthermore, "As the Lord lives, the Lord shall strike him, or his day shall come to die, or he shall go out to battle and perish. The Lord forbid that I should stretch out my hand against the Lord's anointed. But please, take now the spear and the jug of water that are by his head and let us go." So David took the spear and the jug of water by Saul's head and they got away; and no man saw or knew it or awoke. For they were all asleep, because a deep sleep from the Lord had fallen on them.

Now David went over to the other side and stood on the top of a hill afar off, a great distance being between them. And David called out to the people and to Abner the son of Ner, saying, "Do you not answer, Abner?" Then Abner answered and said, "Who are you, calling out to the king?" So David said to Abner, "Are you not a man? And who is like you in Israel? Why then have you not guarded your lord the king? For one of the people came in to destroy your lord the king. This thing that you have done is not good. As the Lord lives, you deserve to die, because you have not guarded your master, the Lord's anointed. And now see where the king's spear is and the jug of water that was by his head."

Then Saul knew David's voice and said, "Is that your voice, my son David?" David said, "It is my voice, my lord, O king." And he said, "Why does my lord thus pursue his servant? For what have I done, or what evil is in my hand? Now therefore, please, let my lord the king hear the words of his servant: If the Lord has stirred you up against me, let Him accept an offering. But if it is the children of men, may they be cursed before the Lord, for they have driven me out this day from sharing in the inheritance of the Lord, saying, 'Go, serve other gods.' So now, do not let my blood fall to the earth before the face of the Lord. For the king of Israel has come out to seek a flea, as when one hunts a partridge in the mountains."

Then Saul said, "I have sinned. Return, my son David. For I will harm you no more, because my life was precious in your eyes this day. Indeed I have played the fool and erred exceedingly." — 1 Samuel 26:5-21

For the second time, David had an opportunity to act in

his own strength against the Lord's anointed. He had the opportunity to avenge himself. But gentleness was his strength under control, so he said, "This man is still the Lord's anointed, even though he did me wrong. I will not touch the Lord's anointed."

This scenario plays out like the previous encounter. David pleads his case. Saul shows signs of repentance, but they still go in opposite directions. And it's good they do, because Saul's apology turns out to be another fake.

Learn the fruit of gentleness from Jesus, who showed us how to use strength under control.

Learn also from David, who used strength under control.

Try as you will to avoid it, some people will do you damage. Even a friend or two might do you wrong. If or when they do, here's the question to ask yourself:

What are you going to do about it?

Will you disrespect them? Is your disrespect justified by their disrespect for you? Didn't Jesus die for them, just like He died for you? Aren't they precious in the Lord's eyes?

God has called us to love and respect even those who are in rebellion to His word and His calling. Respect them because God respects them. You don't have to like people to respect them. You don't have to like the things they do to respect them.

God has given you the fruit of gentleness, which gives you a tremendous strength with control. The strength of gentleness enables you to stand tall in the face of enemies and still love them. You might have every reason in the world to hurt them, but in gentleness you can say, "I'll leave vengeance to the Lord. I'm not going to punish you, although I'm not saying the Lord won't punish you someday. You wronged me but I will respect and honor you. I will also maintain my distance from you, because I may be gentle but I'm not weak. So goodbye."

God is calling you to be strong, not a wimp. He is not calling you to practice carnal strength, as the world would have it. He is calling you to walk in strength with control, so nurture the fruit of gentleness in your life.

Be encouraged by this powerful perspective of a godly character trait that is anything but wimpiness. Nurture the fruit of gentleness by practicing strength under control.

Abide in the Lord and you will bear much fruit!

Self-Control

*But the fruit of the
Spirit is love, joy, peace,
longsuffering, kindness,
goodness, faithfulness,
gentleness and **self-control**.*
— *Galatians 5:22-23*

Each of the nine fruits mentioned by the Apostle Paul in Galatians 5 is unique and essential for rounding out our character as mature and productive followers of Christ. We can't afford to neglect any of the fruit if we hope to prevail over all of life's challenges. In his second epistle, Simon Peter wrote:

Grace and peace be multiplied to you in the knowledge of God and of Jesus our Lord, as His divine power has given to us all things that pertain to life and godliness, through the knowledge of Him who called us by glory and virtue. — 2 Peter 1:2-3

God has given you everything you need for a godly life. If you need a fruit — if you need a character trait or inner resources — know that God has already provided it through Jesus Christ. You only need to know how to tap into the resources God has made available to you. That's why we are taking such great care to unpack each one of these nine fruits of the Spirit. So in this final section, we will delve into the ninth fruit, which is self-control.

Our working definition for self-control has two parts:

Self-control is, first, the ability to restrain our passions and fleshly tendencies; and second, it is the ability to think and behave in ways that are consistent with our goals.

Here we see how the fruit of self-control applies to both negative and positive aspects of character. First, it restrains or holds back the negative tendencies, and second, it nurtures the positive characteristics. With that understanding, let's look at God's intention for cultivating self-control in our lives.

God's Responsibility vs. Our Responsibility

Some believers express confusion over the phrase "self-control." Specifically, they have a problem with the term "self." "If our goal is to submit all things to the Lord," they ask, "why isn't this the fruit of 'spirit-control'? Why would we want our sinful self to control anything? Aren't we called to die to self?"

That's a good question. We need to understand, first, that if God Himself is asking us to cultivate the fruit of self-control, then it is unquestionably a positive thing. If God endorses it, it must be good. The next thing to note is that there are some things that only God can and will do in our lives. Other things He delegates to us. If we don't take charge of the things He delegates to us, He won't do those things for us. Those things are *our* responsibility, not His.

There are, in fact, some things that only God can do. These include our salvation and the empowerment of the Holy Spirit. We can't redeem ourselves. We can't forgive our own sins. These are things that God does for us.

But in many areas of the Christian life, God is not like a kindergarten teacher, holding our hands and guiding our moves. He delegates. He gives us responsibility. He gives us the gifts and passions and abilities to do the things He calls us to do, but He doesn't do these things for us. That's why we need to cultivate self-control. That's why we need to restrain negative tendencies and reinforce positive ones. We do these things because God won't do them for us.

Unfortunately, there is a "super-spiritual" kind of Christian who acts like the Holy Spirit is supposed to do everything for them. They are often paralyzed and unproductive, waiting for God to show up and take control. They are constantly asking God to make His will evident. But the fact is He already has! In His word, He makes it clear that it's *our job* to get His work on earth done. He's already set up the parameters for that work. He has already called, equipped and challenged His people.

So don't sit around saying, "Please, God. What are you going to do about this?" Instead, hear God saying, "I already showed you how to act in love and obedience to my word. You have everything you need. So what are *you* going to do about this?"

When you are faced with a difficult decision, first ask

God for wisdom.

Second, take advantage of every resource He has already given you.

Third, find the self-control and disciple to execute the responsibilities He has placed before you.

But above all, don't do nothing! Act in the wisdom, love and authority that He has entrusted to you.

Without God, we can't do some things; but without us, God won't do some things.

Seven Things God Does for Us

1) God convicts us.

"When He has come, He will convict the world of sin and of righteousness and of judgment." — John 16:8

When we were saved, God brought to our spirits conviction. We did not convict ourselves. Only God has the ability to bring to our awareness the depravity of sin. Only He convicts.

2) God leads us.

As many as are led by the Spirit of God, these are the sons of God. — Romans 8:14

Thank God that we are not responsible for the master plan. His word provides us with the road map. His Spirit leads us toward righteousness and holiness.

3) God intercedes for us.

Likewise the Spirit also helps in our weaknesses. For we do not know what we should pray for as we ought, but the Spirit Himself makes intercession for us with groanings which cannot be uttered. — Romans 8:26

Thank God for the Spirit's intercession! His prayers are above and beyond our own prayers, which we are still obligated to do. The Apostle Paul said:

I will pray with the spirit and I will also pray with the understanding. I will sing with the spirit and I will also sing with the understanding. — 1 Corinthians 14:15b

We like to pray with understanding, having specific action points to lay out before the Lord. But when we don't know how to pray, the Spirit Himself intercedes for us. That's when we cry out to God saying, "Good Lord, I don't even know what to pray for! I need help, so please intercede for me." That's a prayer that the Holy Spirit is happy to answer.

4) God sanctifies us.

... because God chose you as first-fruits to be saved through the sanctifying work of the Spirit and through belief in the truth. — 2 Thessalonians 2:13b (NIV)

The word "sanctified" conjures up images of saints with pious faces wearing white robes and speaking sanctimonious King James English. That's not what sanctified means. Sanctified means being set apart for God's exclusive use. God forgives our sins and sets us apart from the ungodliness of the world. He makes us peculiar people, not falling into the common sins and practices of the world. We can't live right and do good deeds by ourselves, so the Holy Spirit sanctifies us.

5) God comforts us.

Then the churches throughout all Judea, Galilee and Samaria had peace and were edified. And walking in the fear of the Lord and in the comfort of the Holy Spirit, they were multiplied. — Acts 9:31

This verse speaks of a comfort that can only come from heaven. There are times when nothing anybody can say will comfort us. This is the kind of comfort I needed recently when my god-daughter died unexpectedly at an early age. You, too, have felt that kind of heartbreak. At certain times of grief, you have nowhere to turn but to the Lord. He, alone, has the ability to comfort us when our grief is that profound.

6) God empowers us.

"But you shall receive power when the Holy Spirit has come upon you; and you shall be witnesses to me in Jerusalem and in all Judea and Samaria and to the end of the earth." — Acts 1:8

This is the kind of power that no living person can drum up themselves. Empowerment has to come from the Holy Spirit.

7) God gives spiritual gifts.

There are different kinds of gifts but the same Spirit distributes them. — 1 Corinthians 12:4 (NIV)
The Holy Spirit is the giver of spiritual gifts like prophecy, healing and words of wisdom. We cannot pick

and choose them, as if we were browsing through the aisles of a supermarket. Only God gives spiritual gifts.

These are seven things that only God can do. In the next section, we will look at some of the things that God will not do for us. Yes, He will help us do these things, but He will not do them for us. That's why we need to cultivate the fruit of self-control in our lives.

Restraining Passions and Fleshly Tendencies

As we have seen, self-control is, *first, the ability to restrain our passions and fleshly tendencies*. That's the first part of a two-part definition. This truth is unpacked earlier in Galatians 5, the same chapter that lists the fruit of the Spirit.

> *I say then: Walk in the Spirit and you shall not fulfill the lust of the flesh. For the flesh lusts against the Spirit and the Spirit against the flesh and these are contrary to one another, so that you do not do the things that you wish.* — Galatians 5:16-17

In this passage, Paul explains how the flesh and the Spirit are continually opposing each other. It's a constant war between the Spirit and the flesh, as your desires pull you away from where God wants you to be. This is a fact of the spiritual life. The flesh wars against God's intentions. There is constant warfare going on in your heart and mind and spirit.

As we consider spiritual warfare, know that not all warfare is the same. We do not always fight against demons. The Apostle Paul wrote:

*For we do not wrestle against flesh and blood, but
against principalities, against powers, against the
rulers of the darkness of this age, against spiritual
hosts of wickedness in the heavenly places.* —
Ephesians 6:12

Demons are definitely real. They aren't a figment of
people's imagination. But that kind of spiritual warfare is
not what Paul is talking about in Galatians 5. That's why
self-control is included in the fruit of the Spirit. Self-control
is needed to discipline the flesh, not demons. Self-control is
necessary to restrain your carnal passions.

See what Paul says in the verse immediately after he
lists all nine fruits:

*And those who are Christ's have crucified the flesh with
its passions and desires.* — Galatians 5:24

Notice that we are instructed to crucify the flesh. Paul
didn't tell us to crucify demons because he knew that
would be impossible! Don't get it backwards:

*We crucify the flesh and we rebuke demons.
We do not rebuke the flesh and crucify demons.*
Don't get it backwards. Not all battles are with demons.
Some are with the flesh, which must be crucified. As it says
in Galatians 5:17, the flesh is continually warring against
the Spirit. In this battle, you will get nowhere saying to the
flesh, "I rebuke you in the name of Jesus." That's using the
wrong weapon. The "rebuking" weapon may work over
principalities and powers and rulers of darkness, but not
over the flesh. The flesh will not respond to a rebuke.
That's why you need self-control.

When God saved us, He didn't save our flesh, which is constantly at war with the Spirit. The Bible says that "the flesh is hostile to God, for it does not submit to God's law; indeed, it cannot" (Romans 8:7). This is our Adamic nature, shaped after Adam's image. God did not come to save the flesh but to crucify it and to give us a completely new nature.

The Apostle Paul explains in his first letter to the Corinthians:

Not all flesh is the same ... There are also heavenly bodies and there are earthly bodies; but the splendor of the heavenly bodies is one kind and the splendor of the earthly bodies is another ... So will it be with the resurrection of the dead. The body that is sown is perishable, it is raised imperishable; it is sown in dishonor, it is raised in glory; it is sown in weakness, it is raised in power; it is sown a natural body, it is raised a spiritual body.

If there is a natural body, there is also a spiritual body. So it is written: "The first man Adam became a living being"; the last Adam, a life-giving spirit. The spiritual did not come first, but the natural and after that the spiritual. The first man was of the dust of the earth; the second man is of heaven. As was the earthly man, so are those who are of the earth; and as is the heavenly man, so also are those who are of heaven. And just as we have borne the image of the earthly man, so shall we bear the image of the heavenly man. — 1 Corinthians 15:39-49 (NIV)

Our second nature is born in the image of Jesus, who in this passage is called "the last Adam, a life-giving spirit," and "the heavenly man." So while salvation was immediate when we put our trust in Jesus, our flesh was not saved and transformed. We are instructed to constantly put down the Adamic tendency and continually practice self-control and crucify the sinful flesh.

This is warfare, but not the kind of spiritual warfare we read about earlier. It's a significant effort that amounts to war against the flesh to crucify its passions and desires.

Notice how in Galatians 5:24, Paul uses the past tense. "I *have crucified* the flesh with its passions and desires." Does that mean it's all finished, that you're good to go, once and for all?

No! When you are saved, your sinful flesh doesn't die once and for all. If it was literally dead, you couldn't sin if you tried. This is not a once-and-for-all crucifying of the flesh, even though it might sound as if it is. Think of this as a *process* of "staying crucified," of using self-control to "keep your flesh underfoot." This is a process of continually crucifying the flesh, minute by minute by minute. This is the process of continually restraining your passions and fleshly tendencies. This is self-control.

So the first part of cultivating the fruit of self-control is to understand that we have a responsibility to restrain our passions and fleshly tendencies. God won't restrain them for us.

Paul writes in the book of Romans:

... reckon yourselves to be dead indeed to sin but alive to God in Christ Jesus our Lord. Therefore do not let

*sin reign in your mortal body, that you should obey it in
its lusts.* — Romans 6:11-12

Our assignment is clear. We are instructed to say "no"
to fleshly passions and desires. This is something we do,
not something God does for us. The fruit of self-control
empowers us to succeed in this struggle. Sin wants to rule
our mortal bodies but self-control says to the flesh, "Uh-uh.
Your reign is over. I do not obey your lusts anymore. With
the power and strength and authority that God has given
me, I choose to say 'no' to fleshly passions and desires. I
choose self-control over flesh-control."

In truth, the only alternative to "self-control" is "flesh-
control." By default, if you are not practicing self-control,
you are relinquishing your God-given responsibilities to the
flesh. An unrestrained life that is out of control is a train
wreck waiting to happen. In His mercy, God has given us
the means to harness and rein in our desires. He offers us
the beautiful fruit of self-control, which leads to life and
purpose and fulfillment.

Flesh-Control vs. Self-Control

Self-control enables us to live by godly decisions and
values, rather than by fleshly passions and desires. It
enables us to harness what would otherwise be unrestrained
desires. It brings our desires under the authority of God's
Spirit. It makes us more Christ-like. As we become more
like Christ, our areas of weakness begin to stand out in
contrast to His godly standards. The practice of self-control
will highlight areas that are out of control and in need of
discipline.

What are some of the unrestrained practices that scripture warns against? Paul lists some of the works of the flesh in Galatians 5:

Now the works of the flesh are evident, which are: adultery, fornication, uncleanness, lewdness, idolatry, sorcery, hatred, contentions, jealousies, outbursts of wrath, selfish ambitions, dissensions, heresies, envy, murders, drunkenness, revelries and the like; of which I tell you beforehand, just as I also told you in time past, that those who practice such things will not inherit the kingdom of God. — Galatians 5:19-21

These works of the flesh are in stark contrast to the fruit of the Spirit, which are listed immediately afterward. You may have been deep into the works of the flesh before you came to Christ, but now hear God saying, "It's time to crucify all those fleshly practices. Let them die by practicing the fruit of self-control. That's why I'm giving you this gift, so you can learn how to walk in purity. I will teach you how to rein in your desires."

In case you haven't noticed, you didn't drop all your desires off at the altar when you got saved. You became a new creation in Christ but your soul and spirit walked away from that altar chained to your old flesh. And if you don't crucify that flesh on a regular basis, it will start to act as if you never got saved. You know that's true, even with your big Bible and sanctified language!

Your flesh says, "I don't care that you went to the altar. That's between you and God. Now let me tell you why these works of the flesh are so important …"

The flesh still wants to run things, so we have to yield to the Holy Spirit. We have to cultivate love, joy, peace, long-suffering, kindness, goodness, faithfulness, gentleness and self-control. We have to become more like Christ.

The Practical Applications of Self-Control

Let's make this discussion about self-control even more practical now ... and a bit more uncomfortable for some people. Suppose an attractive somebody comes spinning into your orbit. You feel the attraction. Your orbs start to connect and before long, you're being pulled into each other's gravity. All that while, you've known you could put on the brakes — you could have exercised some self-control — but now you feel as if you're falling. You are falling into "the works of the flesh, which include adultery, fornication, uncleanness" and more.

This is not the time to call out to heaven, saying, "God, what is your will here?" This decision is not under His jurisdiction. It is your decision! You don't have to hear God speak from heaven because He already made His will perfectly clear. He already said, "Avoid sexual immorality. I have given sex as a wonderful gift to men and women in the God-ordained context of monogamous marriage until death. Now do you have any other questions?"

You can't make up your own definitions. Shacking up is not marriage. Living together is not a lifelong commitment. The word is crystal-clear. Sex outside of the context of God-sanctioned marriage is wrong, so when you are tempted, practice self-control and crucify the flesh.

The same is true with every sin and work of the flesh mentioned in God's word. Scripture is very practical and very clear. The flesh wants to control and compromise and justify, but the Spirit simply says, "No" to the works of the flesh. Learn to walk in the Spirit and the Spirit will help lead you to joy and purity and life and beauty. Jesus sent a Helper, which is the Holy Spirit. Whether you feel as if you are falling or not, take the Help that's offered to you. You are not strong enough on your own, but with the Spirit's fruit of self-control, you can be more than a conqueror.

In the chapter on Faithfulness, we saw what a faithful servant Joseph was in Egypt. The Lord blessed him to be the chief servant in Potiphar's house. But Joseph was also a young man with certain distinguishing qualities that did not go unnoticed by Sister Potiphar. Here's how the story goes:

Now Joseph was handsome in form and appearance. And it came to pass after these things that his master's wife cast longing eyes on Joseph and she said, "Lie with me." But he refused and said to his master's wife, "Look, my master does not know what is with me in the house and he has committed all that he has to my hand. There is no one greater in this house than I, nor has he kept back anything from me but you, because you are his wife. How then can I do this great wickedness and sin against God?" So it was, as she spoke to Joseph day by day, that he did not heed her, to lie with her or to be with her.
But it happened about this time, when Joseph went into the house to do his work and none of the men of the house was inside, that she caught him by his garment, saying, "Lie with me." But he left his garment in her hand and fled and ran outside. And so it was, when she

saw that he had left his garment in her hand and fled outside, that she called to the men of her house and spoke to them, saying, "See, he has brought in to us a Hebrew to mock us. He came in to me to lie with me and I cried out with a loud voice. And it happened, when he heard that I lifted my voice and cried out, that he left his garment with me and fled and went outside."

So she kept his garment with her until his master came home. Then she spoke to him with words like these, saying, "The Hebrew servant whom you brought to us came in to me to mock me; so it happened, as I lifted my voice and cried out, that he left his garment with me and fled outside."
So it was, when his master heard the words which his wife spoke to him, saying, "Your servant did to me after this manner," that his anger was aroused. Then Joseph's master took him and put him into the prison, a place where the king's prisoners were confined. And he was there in the prison. — Genesis 39:6b-20

So here is Sister Potiphar, a fine and wealthy sister, hitting on Joseph, a strong and handsome young man. He had every fleshly reason to give in. He had been sold out by his own family. He was in a place far removed from the people of God. But he understood his responsibility to Brother Potiphar. He also understood his spiritual obligation, saying "How then could I do such a wicked thing and sin against God?"

With God's strength, Joseph put his self-control into practice. He said "No," but more importantly, he *meant* "No!" There's a huge difference between saying it and meaning it. People like Sister Potiphar hear that first "No" and think, "Uh-huh. I've heard this before. But I have quite a few tricks left in my bag." When she kept trying, God kept giving Joseph the ability to say "No" and mean it.

Notice how Sister Potiphar struck when she knew none of the other servants were around. You may feel weak and alone when the enemy strikes but you are never alone. Your Helper, the Holy Spirit, is your constant companion, enabling you to say "No" and mean it.

The Holy Spirit wants to help you with things like lying. Habitual liars get so used to it, they can't tell truth from lies anymore. The Bible tells us to "speak the truth in love" (Ephesians 4:15). The fruit of self-control is very practical in areas like this, teaching us to not lie but to speak the truth in love. When you see a lie about to come out of your mouth, the Holy Spirit will say, "Nope. Stop right in the middle of that sentence and tell those folk the truth." Or if the lie just dropped out of your mouth, the Spirit says, "You know that wasn't true. Take the chance right now to make it right and tell them what really happened." That's how practical self-control is. It may seem embarrassing, but it's better to swallow your pride than to keep living by the works of the flesh. The Holy Spirit is right with you, teaching you how to walk in godliness.

The fruit of self-control can help you in every area of temptation. It's also instructive in areas that are not necessary sinful, like your spending habits. In the chapter on Faithfulness, we talked about the freedom and joy that comes from exercising self-control at the mall. Don't buy it just because you want it. This may not be your season for spending, especially if it puts you in debt. It may be your season to tell your friends, "Sorry, I can't go out to that restaurant with you all, but how about a walk in the park? Or we could meet at one of our houses for coffee." Even your tithes and offerings require self-control. If you leave your finances under the control of your flesh, you will end up in a world of trouble.

Good health takes self-control. What are you doing with your diet and exercise? Are you being a good steward with the only human body you will ever get? If you are tired of being sluggish and unable to get into your clothes, reach into God's cluster of fruit and pick the one He has provided for your success. He has already answered your prayers for help. He is saying, "Yes! I want you to have more energy. Yes! I can help you wear those clothes in the back of your closet. Yes! I can help get you more excited about a healthy lifestyle."

I know what it's like. I got so tired of going into my closet and praying for a word of knowledge as to what I could wear. I was tired of being tired, of being lethargic all the time and feeling burned out. When I called out to the Lord for help, He reminded me of the help He had already given me through the fruit of self-control. He gave me the strength and wisdom to use that fruit in my life.

You can see now how the practical applications of self-control are extremely diverse. Self-control applies to areas of sin like adultery and lying and stealing and lust. It applies to self-destructive areas like addiction and abuse and critical attitudes. It applies to spiritual growth issues like prayer and personal study. It applies to faith issues like tithing and trusting. It applies to relational issues like marriage and friends and family. It applies to practical areas like finances and health and wellness.

We have seen how God has delegated these things to us. They are not areas of God-control, but self-control. We cannot rebuke these issues in the name of Jesus and expect things to get better. The path before us is much more practical than that. It's more simple. We simply need to exercise self-control.

I'm not saying you should leave God out of these areas! Of course, you ought to draw near to Him and pray continually.

Ask God for strength.
Ask Him for wisdom.
Pray for success.
Seek the support of friends and family.

But do not cry out to God like a helpless victim, saying, "God, why aren't you fixing all these areas of my life?!" God has not given you a spiritual magic wand. Some things just take sweat and perseverance and a generous portion of self-control.

Self-control is a broad category. Everything that God has entrusted to you falls under this blanket. Don't think that God doesn't care, because He does care. He is in touch with every little detail of your life, but He doesn't run every detail. He says, "I want to bless you. I want to help you, so that's why I've given you the Holy Spirit, your helper, who comes alongside to get you where you need to go. That's why I've given you this amazing and powerful fruit of the Spirit."

Cultivate the ninth fruit of the Spirit, which is self-control.

Abide in the Lord and you will bear much fruit!

Fruit for the Harvest

I hope and pray that this study has increased your desire to cultivate the fruit of the Spirit in all areas of your life. God has blessed each one of us with gifts and talents and passions, but we can't just be people with gifts. We have to know how to use these gifts with love, kindness, self-control and every quality mentioned here. We will not win the world to Christ with our giftedness alone. We will not win the world by being the best and loudest singers and praisers of God. We will win the world with our ripe and mature spiritual fruit. That's how God wants to bless the lost, through our fruit.

What is the first step in establishing God's fruit in our lives? The first step is to *abide in Jesus.*

> *"Abide in me and I in you. As the branch cannot bear fruit of itself unless it abides in the vine, neither can you unless you abide in me. I am the vine, you are the branches. He who abides in me and I in him bears much fruit; for without me you can do nothing."* —
> John 15:1-5

Does that excite you like it excites me! Followers of Christ have an incredible purpose and vision! In the past, we may have been without purpose, until the Heavenly

Father stepped into the room and said, "Hey daughter! Hey son! We have an exciting day ahead of us. You and I are going to work in the vineyard together! Stay close to me and we'll grow some delicious and nourishing fruit!"

Count me in!

Let's bear fruit together, for the good of our neighbors and to the praise and glory of our Lord.

Abide in the Lord and you will bear much fruit.

As we are "transformed into His image with ever-increasing glory" (2 Corinthians 3:18; NIV), we receive power to transform the world with the fruit of the Spirit that God has given us. To review, these are the nine character traits listed collectively as the *fruit of the Spirit* in Galatians 5:

AGAPE LOVE *is the purely motivated resolve to think and act in the other person's best interest.*

The Greek language has three different words for love. The word *agape* that's used to describe godly love is nothing like the word we use for infatuation or "falling in love." It's the kind of love that Jesus had when He went to the cross to save us from hell. *Agape* love is supernatural. It comes from God who *is love*. It is selfless. It consciously thinks and acts in other people's best interest. *Agape* love is steadfast and sacrificial.

JOY *is gladness that doesn't require positive circumstances.*

We talked about how joy is superior to happiness. While happiness comes and goes with circumstances, God makes available to us a joy that is steadfast through the ups and downs of life. His joy will carry us through all of life's trials. Joy will even make us look better, feel better, reduce stress, increase our health and lengthen our lives. We looked at a number of very practical ways to increase both happiness and joy.

PEACE *is inner calm and wellbeing, no matter the* *circumstances.*

Like joy, the fruit of peace is not based on circumstances. All hell may be breaking out in our lives and God can still provide a peace that surpasses all understanding. Our neighbors will be drawn to the Lord when they see us display that supernatural peace in the midst of the storms of life. We studied the prerequisites of peace from Philippians 4, which include joy, gentleness, prayer and a mind stayed on God.

LONGSUFFERING *is, first, patience and* *contentment despite irritations, inconveniences and* *inactivity; and second, the ability to put up with other* *people even when they're doing wrong, being difficult or* *causing provocation.*

Longsuffering is especially important for helping us deal with troublesome people in a godly manner. One of the key elements behind longsuffering is to be proactive and remain in Christ, the vine, before challenges arise. We take responsibility for things that are within our "circle of influence." We don't worry about things that are outside of our "circle of influence," but rather submit these concerns to the Lord in prayer.

KINDNESS *is benevolence in action.*

We are connected to a kind vine who wants us to experience His kindness so we can pass it on to others. No fruit is clearer in the life of Jesus than kindness, especially as He expressed love to some of the most ostracized members of society. He called out the lack of kindness within the religious community. He showed us how to befriend sinners. God wants to bring lost souls into His family with kindness, but He won't do it alone. He needs you and me to show His kindness to the world.

GOODNESS *is openhearted generosity toward others, above what we think they deserve.*

We do good things because we have a good, good God. Jesus went around being generous toward others, even when they didn't deserve it. Goodness is a sibling to kindness, but it differs from kindness in that it is deeper, reflecting the inner goodness of the heart. It reflects an authentic openheartedness and generosity of the heart. The fruit of goodness is mindful to pay it forward, not only rejoicing in blessings received, but paying that goodness forward to others.

FAITHFULNESS *is trustworthiness in relationships, responsibilities and resources.*

Faithfulness is the ability to finish what we started. It means keeping our word and being trustworthy in relationships, in responsibilities and in resources. It means keeping our commitments to spouses and friends and coworkers. It means keeping our commitments to God.

GENTLENESS *is strength under control.*

Gentleness doesn't mean weakness. The followers of Jesus are not called to be wimps. The fruit of gentleness is a beautiful strength that is quiet and controlled. Sometimes it's not quiet, but it is always controlled. It works in concert with all the other gifts, like love and kindness and goodness. We saw how a righteous person acting in gentleness can be both terrifying and protective at the same time, like the strong man or woman who will nurture and protect the most vulnerable child.

SELF-CONTROL *is, first, the ability to restrain our passions and fleshly tendencies; and second, it is the ability to think and behave in ways that are consistent with our goals.*

We saw how there are certain things that only God can do, like convicting us of sin and saving us. Conversely, there are things that God chooses *not* to do, but instead He gives us the fruit of self-control so that we can handle them. We studied the tremendous diversity of self-control, how it applies to good habits, bad habits, finances, health, relationships, spiritual habits, things that are sinful and things that are not sinful. Self-control empowers us to crucify the flesh, which is in constant opposition to the Spirit of God in our lives. We are not powerless as long as we exercise the fruit of self-control.

God sets you up for Success

But the fruit of the Spirit is love, joy, peace,
longsuffering, kindness, goodness, faithfulness,
gentleness and self-control. Against such there is no
law. — Galatians 5:22-23

God is the giver of every good and perfect gift.
Through these wonderful fruits, I can hear God saying, "I
love you. I care about you. I'm setting you up for success. I
want you to enjoy victory. I want you to experience life to
the fullest."

Jesus had much to say about experiencing a fruitful and
abundant life, which is in stark contrast to the life that the
enemy would want you to have:

"The thief does not come except to steal and to kill and
to destroy. I have come that they may have life and that
they may have it more abundantly." — John 10:10

An abundant life is one that will bear much fruit. The
vineyard is a place brimming with so much life, you can
hardly contain it. Our good Gardener has equipped us with
everything we need to bear much fruit. He calls us to
remember that this fruit is not just to bless believers. Yes,
the fruit will bless us immensely, but it is intended to bless
other people as well. We can't have a proper party when
some people in the neighborhood are still hungry. Open up
and let them see your fruit. Invite them in. Say, "Come into
the orchard! Grab some fruit. There's plenty here to share!"
Their lives will be forever blessed because of your fruit.

That is God's intention for every believer. He has

endowed us with rich spiritual characteristics that reflect His image and His glory. He gives us spiritual fruit to match every deficit that the world will ever experience. Impatient people will see our patience and say, "Hmm. What do they have that I don't have?" Hateful people will come along and say, "Where do they get that love from? I want some." Anxious people will see the peace of God that surpasses all human understanding and say, "Wow! I need some of that." They will see all of God's luscious fruit in our lives and say, "Tell me more about the fruit that's hanging on your vine. I'm hungry. I need what you have."

Even David in the Old Testament had a picture of God's fruit when he said:

Oh, taste and see that the Lord is good. — Psalm 34:8a

Today is a great day to offer that invitation to your neighbors. "Taste and see that the Lord is good!" Thankfully, you don't have to wave a big black Bible at them to show them. You only have to show them your lives! Let them sample some of the fruit from the vine. Be loving and generous toward them. Encourage them in their weakness. Bring them joy when they're down.

Then when they are ready, help them with their own gardens. Show them how they can get some of this fruit growing in their own lives. Share your testimony, because there's no more powerful defense of the Gospel than a changed life. Help them get grafted into the Vine. Show them how all their deepest yearnings are satisfied in Christ.

There is no greater testimony of God's grace than a life

that is bursting with His amazing fruit. That is our ultimate purpose in life. When folk say, "Nice fruit," we can say, "But you should have seen me ten or twenty years ago. I was angry. I was unloving. I was impatient. But God in His mercy has done a piece of work on me. I'd love to tell you more about it, but first … can I get you something to drink? Are you hungry? Are you hurting? How can I show you some kindness?"

Abide in the Lord and you will bear much fruit!

~ ~ ~ ~ ~

Because we all need to build stronger character, I invite you to pray this prayer from your heart:

Dear God, thank you for loving me, saving me, and promising to complete the good work you began in me. I acknowledge my need for genuine fruit, and I ask You to make me more like Jesus, that others will see His life, love, and character in me. Bless me and make me a blessing to everyone I meet. I ask these things in the matchless name of Jesus,   *Amen*

APPENDIX

Galatians 5:22 in Greek[13]

But the fruit	καρπὸς (karpos)	2590: fruit
of the Spirit	πνεύματος (pneumatos)	4151: wind, spirit
is love,	ἀγάπη (agapē)	26: love, goodwill
joy,	χαρὰ (chara)	5479: joy, delight
peace,	εἰρήνη (eirēnē)	1515: peace
patience (long-suffering),	μακροθυμία (makrothumia)	3115: patience, long-suffering
kindness,	χρηστότης (chrēstotēs)	5544: goodness, excellence, uprightness
goodness,	ἀγαθωσύνη (agathōsunē)	19b: goodness
faithfulness,	πίστις (pistis)	4102: faith, faithfulness

---

[13] Including Strong's Concordance numbers, from: James Strong, *Strong's Concordance*, 1890, Public Domain.

Made in the USA
Columbia, SC
20 November 2021